CONFIRMATORY
ANALYSIS®: FINDING
WINNING STOCKS

CONFIRMATORY ANALYSIS®: FINDING WINNING STOCKS

Richard J. Davis, M.D., M.B.A.
James E. Farris, Ed.D.
Allan P. Harris, J.D.

Writers Club Press
San Jose New York Lincoln Shanghai

Confirmatory Analysis®: Finding Winning Stocks

Writers Club Press
an imprint of iUniverse, Inc.

For information address:
iUniverse, Inc.
5220 S. 16th St., Suite 200
Lincoln, NE 68512
www.iuniverse.com

ISBN: 0-595-20129-6

Printed in the United States of America

Trademarks

All terms mentioned in this book that are known to be trademarks or service marks have been appropriately capitalized. Use of a term in this book should not be regarded as affecting the validity of any trademark or service mark. Confirmatory Analysis®, PFT ELS®, One Page Research® are registered trademarks of Richard J. Davis, M.D., M.B.A.

To Dave Zawicki (1953-2000)
"Tech Guru"
gurus@intrepid.com

Dave was a dear and close personal friend of all of the authors of this book. We came to know him through our Internet group, gurus@intrepid.com. Over the years, we developed a very close camaraderie with Dave, based on common interests in both technology and investing.

His knowledge base in technology was second to none. Dave always freely shared his expertise with everyone in our *guru* group. Not surprisingly, many of us benefitted from our exchange of information with him over the Net.

Throughout Dave's illness and early departure from this life, his attitude was consistently optimistic and hopeful. His devoted wife, Carol, was continually by his side, with her strength always sustaining him. She was a true inspiration to all who knew Dave, both virtually, and in person.

As a mentor to us in the group, Dave raised the bar to challenge us, but, was like a brother and friend who encouraged, yet never scolded. Without his personal encouragement in writing this book, it would never have come into existence. Thank you, Dave.

Confirmatory Analysis \ n. the art and science of utilizing *fundamental analysis* to select outstanding growth and value stocks coupled with *technical analysis* to *identify* potentially winning stocks using the Internet.

Contents

Preface

At present, it takes less time for technologies to gain wide acceptance in the public sector than in prior recorded history. Certainly, not all varieties of technology are adopted and become integrated into the mainstream. A 25% adoption rate, in fact, is considered to be a benchmark for success. The Internet is an example of such a successful technology and has become the enabling communication vehicle for the new millennium. Thus, using this book (which in seamlessly integrated into this technology) is contingent upon the user's rapid access to information from the Net and his/her ability to make informed decisions about stocks. Other successful non Web-based technologies are noted below, yet, none have been adopted and assimilated quicker by the public than the Internet.

Technology	Year Invented	Years to 25 % Adoption
Electricity	1873	46
Telephone	1876	35
Car	1886	55
Radio	1906	22
TV	1926	26
VCR	1952	34
PC	1975	16
Cellular phone	1983	13
Internet	1991	7

Source: Miliken Institute

Acknowledgements

This book was created from many ideas and concepts produced by the authors. Others from our Internet group, *gurus@intrepid.com*, were instrumental in critiquing our theories and providing invaluable investment insights to our work. Without the formation of the group by Mary Peterson, and use of Gary Funck's servers, the authors would never have met nor ultimately created this book.

We remain indebted to the ongoing support by our wives and families. Doubts arose many times during discussions surrounding this manuscript, but unwavering encouragement was always near at hand.

Special thanks go to Dr. Robert Lum, one of the *gurus@intrepid.com*, whose vision, and expertise allowed me to create financial calculators on the Web.

I am indebted to Suku Ramanathan, another guru from *gurus@intrepid.com*, for his keen wisdom on technology research and investing.

In addition, I would like to extend my sincere appreciation to Nathan Taylor for copy editing the book and providing outstanding Web programming skills in making One Page Research® very user-friendly.

I am also very grateful to Allison Davis for her original graphic design of the book covers, images and text layouts. Lastly, my most sincere appreciation is also extended to Dr. Pattie Davis-Wiley for her meticulous efforts in enhancing the present manuscript for readability while serving as a visiting scholar-professor in South Korea.

Dr. Richard Davis

Chronology

1994   The *gurus@intrepid.com*, an Internet investing group, is virtually born on the Web.

1995   Authors meet in cyberspace on the list server.

1996   **Fast Company** magazine runs article in June about the group called, *"The Smartest Stock Pickers in Cyberspace."*

1997   Dick Davis and Allan Harris first met in person and begin screening stocks in Kiawah Island, SC using fundamental and technical analysis.

1998   Confirmatory Analysis® and PFT ELS® are born.

1999   Initial topics for book are discussed. Jim Farris joins the book team. Dave Zawicki's expert knowledge and skills allow *www.confirmatoryanalysis.com* to go live.

2000   One Page Research® evolves as Internet stock research tool.

2001   Book completed.

Introduction

The authors hope the title and cover of this book caught your eye and interest with a few standout examples in an otherwise homogeneous array of bright, shiny, highly polished steel cylinders. Similarly, individual investors are always looking for a stock whose price over time rises amidst the crowded universe of over 8,000 individual equities.

Whenever you hear CEOs talk about their respective companies on one of the financial television networks, these spokespersons always talk in positive terms about their companies. They are, after all, hoping to bring new shareholders into their ranks as true believers in the uniqueness of their companies, and the latter's potential for success in the future. Whether you hear CEOs on TV, analysts' commentaries, or your friends around the water cooler talk about a particular stock, how do you *really* know if this is good company to invest in or not? In an attempt to answer this question, this book has been written for the beginning to intermediate investor. Coupled with two *free* Web sites for the reader, the book will serve as an educational tool, allowing one to sharpen his/her analytical skills in understanding key financial characteristics of a company, in addition to how to look at its price chart. Hopefully, using both strategies, investors will be in a better position to decide whether or not they have selected a stock with potential for future growth.

What differentiates winning stocks (red and green) from the crowded field of shiny look-alike cylinders on this book's cover is what the book is all about. We will begin telling a story about the beginning of the journey that began the process of writing this book. Then, the reader will be led to understanding the financial characteristics of a company and evaluating its price chart or technical analysis. Using one stock as an example, we will dissect the process of establishing Confirmatory Analysis in detail. This will allow the reader to identify fundamentally strong stocks and those with excellent price patterns as potential winning stocks in the world where every stock is shiny and looks similar as in our cover picture.

Two chapters are devoted to the difficult but timely areas of technology investing. One is dedicated to guiding the reader how to identify technology trends and stocks. The other chapter covers in detail PFT ELS, a new financial ratio for analyzing productivity and efficiency of rapidly-growing companies. Using PFT ELS should assist the reader hoping to differentiate similar technology companies within the group or industry sector.

In subsequent chapters, instructions and locations for guiding the investor in the use of stock screening will be covered. After a small but manageable number of stocks have been screened, the final step, *due diligence*, will be covered in detail. Using a step-by-step approach and simple algorithms (i.e., formulae), learning to fully research stocks should become easy for the beginning to intermediate investor. Afterwards, investors should be better able to decide whether or not to purchase a stock or place in a dummy (e.g., hypothetical) portfolio for observation. As a shrewd investor once said, *"…there are no good or bad stocks, only stocks that go up or down."* Learning how to identify those winning stocks is the mission of this book.

Chapter 1

Preparing for the Journey—In the Beginning...

By Richard J. Davis, M.D., M.B.A.
and James E. Farris, Ed.D.

The only way to get the lead and stay in the lead is to be smart and work hard.

-David Ho, M.D. , Aids Researcher

Introduction

In the Beginning...Internet Investment Discussion Group

In order to understand how the authors wrote this book, a little background information should prove helpful. The authors first met through the cyberspace by means of an Internet discussion group identifying themselves as the *Gurus*, and consisting of approximately 40 individuals residing in North America and Europe. The group's common thread was to seek, share and exchange information pertaining to a particular stock, market sector, or the market conditions in general. The *Gurus* were and are a diverse group of individuals who have a passion for investing. All members of the *Gurus* make their own investment decisions, however, they are free to use their fellow members as a sounding board or as a forum for considering the merits of their prospective investment ideas before making a purchase or sell decision for a particular security.

During the quiet moments, the *Gurus* discuss investing ideas. Ideas are quickly analyzed, commented on and either affirmed or negated. To the authors it is reassuring to know that one is not alone and that investing ideas can be tested in close to real-time without the typical distractions and inconveniences of meetings, memos, or even 'phone tag.' A day in the life of the *Gurus* is filled with what they refer to as their 'day job,' the occupation that supports their families and life style, and a relatively small amount of time devoted to investing. With the help of the Internet, smart decisions about stocks can be made in a short period of time because they have been tested in cyberspace.

Out of the larger group of *Gurus*, three individuals formed a subgroup to explore in-depth the potential of Confirmatory Analysis®, PFT ELS®, and One Page Research®. It should be noted that, with the exception of two who live in the same town, the authors rarely conversed over the telephone, and only on one occasion have the authors met and discussed investment ideas and strategies as a group. What makes this story unique is that all three authors are professionals in different occupational fields, including education, medicine, computer science, law, technology and research. Their primary bond is the desire to seek and exchange information, and to test new investment concepts for identifying potentially winning stocks using current and newly created tools on the Internet. As you read this book, you will come to understand the value of using Confirmatory Analysis and other tools readily available to all Internet users. Selecting stocks with the greater knowledge of these tools should reduce investors' downside risk and increase upside potential.

In the Beginning....Ultrak's Story-90 Days In the Life of the Authors

In February of 1996, *Allan Harris* took time to review *Jay Saxena's Growth Stocks Report,* and Louis Navellier's MPT Review (*www.mptreview.com*). These newsletters specialize in quantitative research based on fundamental reasons for stocks to grow. The large number of stocks, each with endless strings of numbers beside them, made it confusing as to which securities Allan should have looked at to consider purchasing. Admittedly, all of those numbers connote the company's fundamentals, but alas, which one to buy? Allan, a lawyer familiar with legal precedent, knows from experience that the first time a stock is printed in either of these newsletters, it will appreciate due to the recommendation of their publishers. His investment goal was finding stocks before Jay, Louis, and others publish them, which would nearly guarantee a successful investment. Once published in either newsletter, these stocks are prone to rise rapidly from the increased investor interest. Allan knew how to recognize patterns in law, so he looked for patterns on the stock charts that might tell him which stock to buy.

On the last weekend in June, 1996, Allan was prospecting in *Investor's Business Daily* (IBD) examining a myriad of stocks, their stories, numbers and graphs. He had compiled a list of promising stocks after looking at their chart patterns in the "Your Weekend Graphic Review" section of IBD. He knew that not all of those stocks were potential gold, but a few of them might be. Suddenly, one stock, ULTRAK, a company in the closed circuit TV manufacturing and monitoring business, captured his attention. (See Figure 1.)

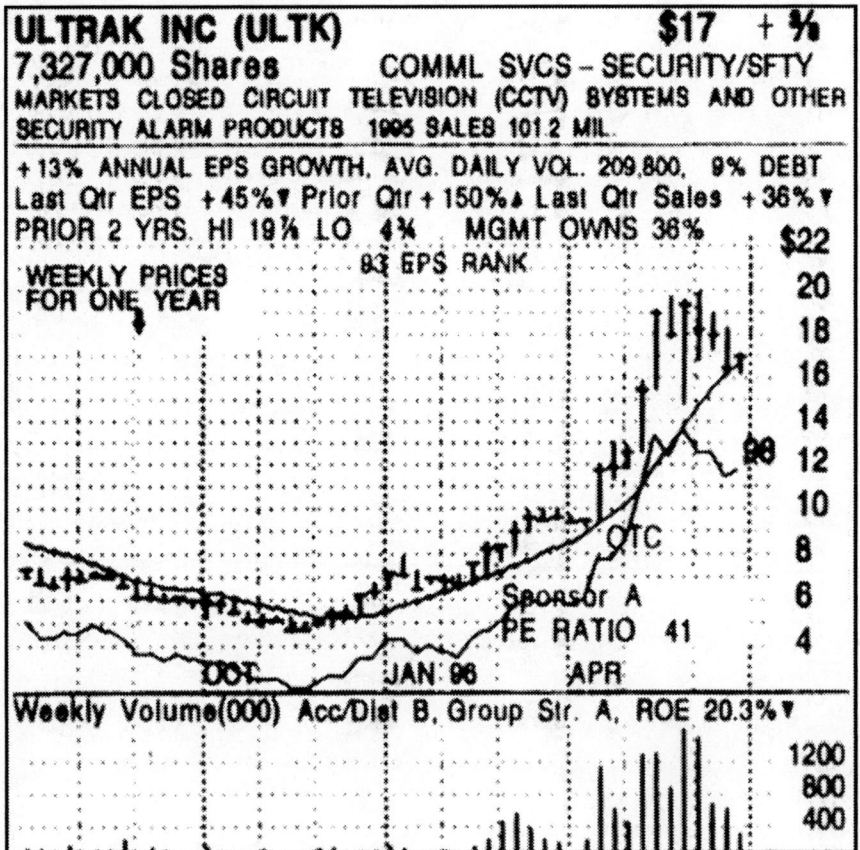

Figure 1. Price chart of Ultrak 6/25/96

Allan noticed the price pattern of ULTK closing at $17 per share, up 5/8. It had a steeply rising trend that had just recently had a mild retracement, i.e., price pull back or downward moves. (See Figure 2 for an example of retracement.)

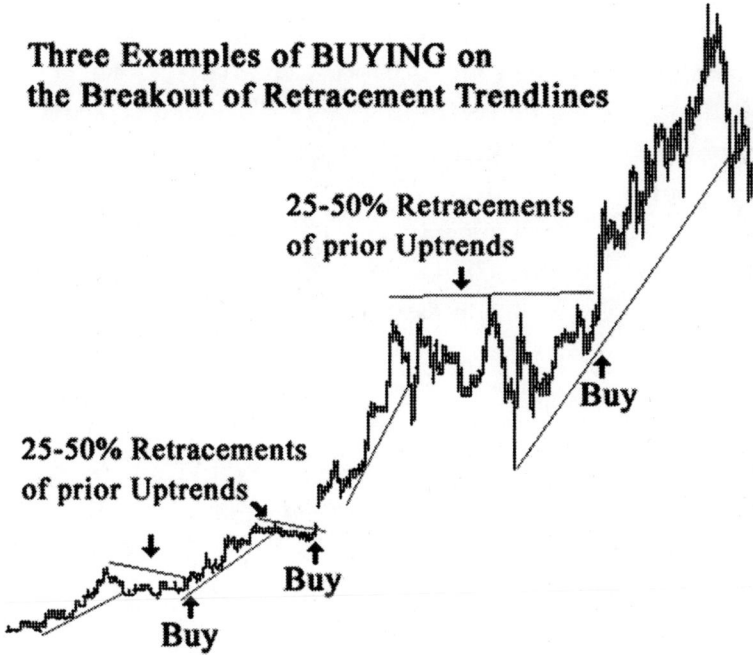

Three Examples of BUYING on the Breakout of Retracement Trendlines

25-50% Retracements of prior Uptrends

25-50% Retracements of prior Uptrends

Buy

Buy

Buy

Figure 2. Ultrak - Buy signals

Allan knew from experience that it is these types of patterns that potentially forecast further upward price movement or appreciation. He asked himself, "Is this the case with ULTK, or is it just reaching the top of its trading range?" Instinctively, he posted a message to the *Gurus* with a list of stocks including ULTK and asked for the group's thoughts.

While reading the Guru weekend e-mail, *Dick Davis* found Allan's post. Like Allan, he was a subscriber to IBD, and Louis Navellier's MPT Review on line as well. Dick was a physician with an M.B.A. who used fundamental analysis to screen stocks, emphasizing on growth and momentum. Having developed a historically tested screening model, Dick inserted the information on ULTK into his fundamental stock screening model to produce a quantitative score. This fundamental model will be explained in detail in a later chapter.

Using Dick's model, ULTK, produced a high fundamental score. When Dick combined his fundamental score with the technical analysis chart Allan had earlier faxed to him, it seemed that the first piece of evidence had been obtained that ULTK was a good candidate to buy. In addition, Allan made the following comments concerning ULTK. "Monday close about $17.5 would be a Buy, with short term targets of $24-30." *This was fewer than 24 hours after the initial e-mail posting about a proposed list of stocks to purchase!* E-mail was posted to the remainder of the *Gurus* by Dick, listing all of Allan's picks with his fundamental scoring of each. Only three out of ten passed the fundamental model, however only *one* out of ten had received two thumbs up. A recommendation to the *Gurus* was made with advice to shadow this stock, or watch it rather than simply buy on either technical or fundamental analysis. On Monday morning, June 30, 1996, Dick Davis placed a purchase order for ULTK. Allan did the same a short time later.

After buying a stock, the purchaser often has some uncertainty whether he/she has made the right decision. Allan commented that buying it at $ 17 per share was okay, but "…a stop loss (a tool to preserve capital when a stock declines) at $ 15 ½ with a target in the mid-20's was acceptable. Not a bad risk/reward trade." Thus establishing the potential downside risk of a $1.50 a share vs. a possible upside gain of $ 7.00 a share. This knowledge helps to put the buyer at ease when buying a new security. On June 30, 1996, ULTK's stock achieved an intra-day high of $18.50, but closed at $18.00.

As the July Fourth holiday weekend approached, *Jim Farris* (another of the authors, and member of the *Gurus*) commented that he felt the conjoint analysis and decision was correct about ULTK. Jim commented that with "*...Allan's short term target of $ 24-30, re-evaluation might be necessary if the stock actually achieved Allan's target projections!*" The stock inched up slightly to close at a 52-week high of $19 7/8 on July 3, 1996. Was there really something to this stock's rise? No news was released, nor was there evidence from earning's announcements. Something was occurring with the company and something was increasing the demand for its stock. Allan and Dick mused about whether the newsletter pundits, Jay Saxena or Louis Navellier, would add ULTK to their recommended list and help the stock appreciate.

Almost without warning in July 1996, a correction hit the high technology sector led by Intel's news of slow demand for their processor chips. Virtually all technology stocks were being reduced in value by 20-25% including big name stocks such as Hewlett Packard and others. Ultrak, as part of the overall tech sector, also suffered from significant volatility on July 16, 1996, with the price trading as low as $12 5/8 to $16 3/8. Although not immune to the pall within the overall sector, this corrective phase was relatively short-lived for Ultrak, and soon the stock began stabilizing in a trading range of $16—$18 per share.

Among the *Gurus*, ULTK served to stimulate a general discussion of the security industry as a whole. Guru *Robert Lum* stated that "*...miniature cameras were nothing new, having been around for awhile. However, the cost had rapidly diminished from installed cost of $5,000 each to the cost-effective price point to be installed in quantity.*" Admittedly, with stickers on virtually every store window indicating the presence of CCTV (closed circuit television), they had become nearly ubiquitous. Since the barriers to entry for security firms were generally low, the point of differentiation that ULTK was taking must have been quite unique to account for its expanding sales, earnings, and price appreciation. It was clear that the security business was competitive, but the question lingered: Why was ULTK so successful while others in similar lines of business were not.

On July 17, 1996, Rienhardt Krause published an article about ULTK in *Investor's Business Daily*. Krause stated in his article that "…(ULTK) had its eye out for the next opportunity." From police applications monitoring the streets of Baltimore to a wireless *BabyCam* (a system for monitoring babies and children), Ultrak was clearly a leader in innovative systems. Ultrak products were clearly *cost effective solutions* to security and monitoring products. They were even marketing a system whereby dentists could educate patients on why treatments may be needed. Heavy investment in research and development resulted in inroads not only into the retailing sector but into the professional and consumer markets with products that were reliable and affordable. Competition from foreign manufacturers producing similar products might seem inevitable, but Ultrak had created a patented system called DAVE, or *D*uplex *A*nalog *V*ideo *E*ncoder system, which made its systems the solution of choice in the surveillance market. DAVE allows "…a large array of cameras connected by a single loop of coaxial cable. Usually, each camera required its own direct wiring to a central location."[1] Ultrak had discovered a way to not only to bring the costs of installation down but to improve surveillance. Who was using Ultrak systems? Wal-Mart, Kinko's, Great Atlantic and Pacific Atlantic and Pacific Tea Company (A&P grocery stores), Rite-Aid, and Eckerd Corporation were just a few of Ultrak's key customers. Other

---

1 Ultrak's Annual Report to shareholders, 1995.

components in the systems came from acquired companies, such as Diamond Corp. and Bissett, a French Company which had developed high-speed dome viewing camera technology. Ultrak's stellar earnings and cash flow allowed them to acquire expertise from around the globe.

Moving into early August, ULTK had begun to trade in a very narrow sideways pattern with daily price movements of only a dollar or so. Some of the *Gurus* were uncertain as to whether the stock had reached its peak price at around $20 a share. Allan was asked to revisit the charts and his analysis revealed that ULTK's technical pattern was now weaker with only a potential rise in the range of $ 22-28. However, the fundamental model score remained unchanged. Another episode of confirmation had occurred despite the volatile price of the stock in July and the doldrums of August. Those *Gurus* owning the stock decided to stay put.

As fate would have it, on Monday August 19, 1996, Louis Navellier's MPT Mid-Month Bulletin placed ULTK in its *Top Buy List Stocks by Projected Earning's Growth*. A few days passed as the U.S. Mail subscribers received the newsletter and discovered ULTK on the list among many other recommended stocks. On August 18, 1996, the stock rose 3 1/8 on five times the average volume. The fundamental numbers posted by Louis Navellier beside ULTK, shared common elements with Dick Davis's fundamental model. (% Change in Quarterly Earnings, ROE %, and % Change in Annual EPS Growth.) Although not completely paralleling the *Guru* model of fundamental screening, another example of Confirmatory Analysis had taken place. This was a happy day for Allan Harris and Dick Davis and any of the other *Gurus* who longed to find a stock under the radar screen of market pundits. They had truly discovered gold. A confirmation had taken place when one of Wall Street's most respected newsletter writers discovered what the *Gurus* had known for some time.

Conclusion

It had been ninety days since Allan Harris first spotted a pattern on a chart among hundreds of graphs and numbers. However, it had been an interesting ninety days for the *Gurus* as they looked at ULTK from many perspectives, all done electronically via the Internet, no voice communication, and an occasional facsimile transferred between Allan Harris and Dick Davis.

The potential importance of Confirmatory Analysis, i.e., combining both Dick Davis's fundamental model with Allan Harris's technical analysis into an investment technique with greater likelihood of upside potential and downside risk parameters, was established. From this first example the authors began to work together to refine and quantify Confirmatory Analysis. Now it's time to begin your journey in exploring Confirmatory Analysis.

The remainder of the book is devoted to an in-depth examination of *fundamental and technical analysis*. Tying these two investment strategies together as one is the key that led to the development of an investing concept trademarked as Confirmatory Analysis. This book will teach you how to use this strategy in a step by step manner to find your own potentially winning stocks.

One of the most difficult tasks as an investor is *really* understanding important fundamental ratios. Hopefully, the information presented here will help you successfully navigate the rapids of volatility, and provide safe passage through the twists and bends of turbulent times on your way to investment success. Again, what is most meaningful will be the decisions which you will make prior to and during your investment journey.

Along your journey, you will learn how to make practical application of Confirmatory Analysis. At various points in the book, the authors will direct you to their interactive web sites at *www.confirmatoryanalysis.com* and *www.onepageresearch.com*. In preparation for your investment journey, the authors will help you gain a grasp of technical analysis through seemingly simple examples and patterns, and demonstrate ways to recognize these patterns as entry and exit points for buying and selling stocks. Certainly, no matter how diligent you are, not all stocks selected will be winners. However, the authors will guide you through the identification of key fundamental criteria, and the use of screening tools available on the Internet. This will reduce your search time and allow the winnowing of a universe of over 8,000 stocks to a more manageable number, making informed decisions possible, and the likelihood of success much greater.

Chapter 2

Technical Analysis in One Lesson

By Allan P. Harris, J.D.

If you understand, things are just as they are;
if you do not understand, things are just as they are.

-Zen proverb

Introduction

At the age of 44, I left my career as a lawyer to devote my full-time efforts to trading stocks for a living. In my mind I had mastered the art of technical analysis, using price patterns alone to determine how to trade stocks. Since I could trade from anywhere that had electricity for my computer and a phone line, I moved my family from the big, burly urbanity of Atlanta, Georgia, to a semi-tropical beach paradise called Kiawah Island, South Carolina. I had the misconception that I was the

King of Technical Analysis, invincible, all-knowing and thoroughly equipped with all the skills needed to navigate the lucrative waters of trading stocks for a living.

Throughout my legal career my real love, or should I say obsession, was the stock market. In particular, I was a technical analysis junkie. I had read every technical analysis book I could find and had purchased and learned just about every complicated technical analysis software program available. I had attended expensive seminars and bought a number of well thought of technical analysis systems. I spent even more hours analyzing charts and esoteric price patterns every day then I ever spent in the practice of law.

Although the work was never done, the analysis never complete, the methodology never all that clear, I surrendered to this greater calling in the fall of 1993. In one tumultuous six month period, I resigned from my law firm, sold my house in Atlanta, packed-up my wife and two young daughters, and moved to the beach. My dream had come true, I was a trader. The only problem was, I didn't know how to trade.

The revelation came about six months after moving to Kiawah. It had been six months of frustrating, mediocre returns that seemed to be the result of random luck as much as successful analysis. After one particularly distressing day of trading, I went for a walk on the beach. It was approaching sunset, not long after the market had closed on a day when I thought a certain pharmaceutical stock was "overpriced." It had gone up relentlessly for several weeks. My indicators were all 'overbought' and screaming for me to short the stock. That morning I did. Half-way into the trading day, trading was halted. This was it, I told myself, the auditors were about to be arrested, or better yet, the company's products seized by the FDA. Fifteen minutes after the close, the company was bought out, for a 25% premium over where I had shorted the stock. I was out about $15,000. Ironically, that was about the same amount of money I had already spent on all those books, computers, software programs, seminars and technical analysis systems.

I'm walking along the beach, thinking of how everything I had come to understand about technical analysis had led me to short this stock, and how all this expensive, sophisticated, time-consuming, brow-beating, up-late-at-night-every-night knowledge could have been so wrong. Who could have seen this coming? Who could have known there was about to be a takeover? Well, for starters, everyone who had been buying the stock the weeks prior to the takeover did. What did *they* know that I didn't?

Well, there was one thing we all knew, one simple, poignant, distinctive characteristic of this 'overbought' and 'screaming to be sold' stock:

We all knew that the stock was going up, day after day after day.

It was public information available to anybody who was watching the stock. My indicators and expensive technical analysis programs knew it. The market knew it. I knew it. What did it all mean? It meant the stock was going up. Nothing more, nothing less. There was nothing 'overpriced' about it. There was no 'overbought' about it. All there was, was a stock that was going up.

So here I am, looking out at the Atlantic ocean, watching these little sandpipers sticking their beaks into the sand pulling up their dinner, then doing it again and again and again. Here I am, watching wave after wave after wave of the sea just coming onto the shore, again and again and again. Here I am, watching this stock go up and up and up, day after day after day, then making my bet that it won't go up again. Bingo!

In a moment that has changed everything for me, I discovered the predictive magic of simple observation.

In the weeks that followed, I began trading anew. My expensive computer programs went unused and not a single oscillator graced my computer screen. I started looking at stocks for the first time, and stopped looking at all the tangential mathematical hyperbole that was and is the heart and soul of traditional store-bought technical analysis. I learned in a moment of watching a beach sandpiper fish for its dinner, the essence of real technical analysis:

Buy stocks that are going up and sell stocks that are going anywhere else.

In the words and ideas that follow, I will set out a simple but powerful technique for buying and selling stocks. It is based almost entirely on causal observation and common sense, two tools that come as standard equipment for most stock market participants. Anyone who can look at a price chart and draw a straight line should be able to master the art of technical analysis, or at least technical analysis as taught to me several years ago by a group of anonymous sandpipers, on a beautiful Atlantic beach.

Technical Analysis Explained—In One Second

Technical analysis is the art of looking at a stock's price history in an attempt to predict that stock's price future. How one looks at then analyzes that price history has been the subject of a myriad of books, treatises, trading systems, software and an entire industry of trading advisories, newsletters and services. It can be as simple as looking at a stock chart or as complicated as measuring the angular geometry between the inner and outer planets of our solar system. I have come a long way, only to rely upon the simple approach. It makes trading, and life much easier.

Let us assume for a moment that you have accepted the proposition that one wants to buy stocks that are going up. Believe it or not, the way to consistently do this, is to indeed *buy stocks that are going up.* Could it be this easy? The first issue to resolve concerns the concept of a stock *going up.* Do we mean by *up*, a stock that is higher today then yesterday? Higher this week then last week? Higher this month then last month? All of the above?

What first appears to present a complicated dilemma is easily resolved. This is technical analysis in one lesson: *If you want to know if a stock is going up, you look at it.* That is to say, you look at a chart of the stock. A chart is merely a graphical representation of a stock's price history. When you are looking at a stock's price history in this fashion, you are in a position to determine if this stock is in fact, *going up.*

There will be one of three possible scenarios for this stock, all represented on the chart: (1) It's going *up*; (2) It's going *down*; or (3) It's going both *up* and *down*, a sophisticated technical analysis concept called "Sideways." The only stocks that we want to buy or own are stocks that are classified in #1, those that are, by a look at their chart alone, going *up*. If it takes you longer then say, one second, to determine if it is going up, throw it out with the losers, it's too complicated to be included.

Here's a test. This page contains a weekly price chart of a mystery stock. (See Figure 1.) Give yourself about one second to determine the direction of this stock. If you live in California, give yourself two seconds to compensate for the time change.

What we have done is applied one of Newton's laws of physics to narrow down the field and selection of investment choices. You will probably not believe this now, but in about twenty years of investing you will come to live by this observation: Whatever a stock price is doing now, is most probably what it will be doing tomorrow, next week and next month. If it is going up now, it most probably will be going up tomorrow, next week and next month. If it is going down now, then its most probable course for the foreseeable future is probably down as well. If it can't make up its mind which way it wants to go, it will probably be just as confused when the sun comes up tomorrow.

How long does it take to determine the direction of this stock?

Figure 1. Price pattern

Note the use of the concept of probability. There are no absolutes when it comes to technical analysis or stock selection. The whole idea of choosing one investment or stock over another is based on probability theory. What is the probable course of that stock's price future? Fundamentalists might use sales and earnings so evaluate probabilities.

Technical analysts use price patterns. The probabilities are that what-ever price direction is in force in the present will continue to be in force in the future. Not completely 100 % sure, just probably.

The Catch—Lesson Two

If it were this easy, all investors would be rich beyond their dreams, all poverty would be vanquished from mankind and all the worlds would be at peace…probably. Here's the catch: Figure 2 shows ***stocks do not go up in a straight line, they zig and zag.***

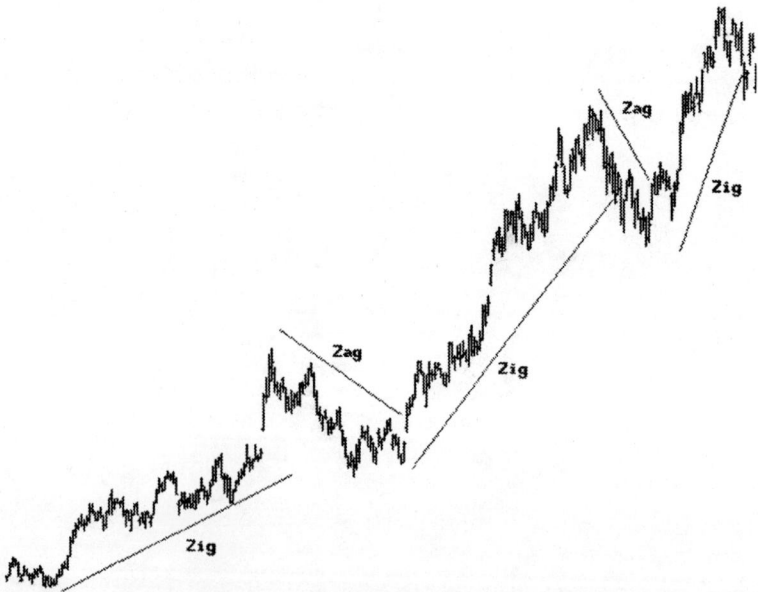

Figure 2. Stock prices zig and zag

Pattern Recognition—Going Up

If there is a single price pattern that best characterizes rising prices, it is the stair-stepped ascending pattern, whereby prices tend to go up for extended periods, turn sideways or down for a short time, then resume their upward climb to still higher levels. Imagine a stock moving up in five-point increments, say from 10 to 15 to 20 to 25, like line markers on a football field. After each five-point increment, it rests, either by staying within a point of the line marker, or by retracing maybe half-way back to the previous marker. At 25, the stock stops moving up and might even fall back down to about 22-23. Imagine a fullback carrying the ball right up the middle of the line, only to be thwarted back for a three-yard loss. It may move back to 25 a second time and again fall back a point or two. In technical terms, 25 is termed *resistance*, likened to a very big, very strong and very angry defensive line. The area where the stock retraces to is termed *support*. Bouncing back and forth between resistance and support affords an opportunity to purchase the stock prior to its next rally through resistance, through 25, on its way to 30 and beyond. In other words, if the trend is strong enough, eventually the offense will prevail and move up the field.

Pattern recognition seeks to identify those stocks that have already seen a sharp rise, are temporarily finding some token resistance at any given price level and are *PROBABLY* ready to fly again. The most telling mark of this kind of price pattern is repetition. The stock has repeatedly risen to resistance, stalled temporarily, then taken off right through resistance. This new move past resistance is termed a *breakout* as the stock *breaks out* above previous highs and signals a dynamic move up to whatever price level becomes the new, albeit temporary, resistance level.

This pattern is what we want to buy. It has all the characteristics we are looking for: A stock that's moving up and a stock that is providing zigs and zags that are always followed by new highs. Reading the zigs and zags correctly tells us when to jump on board and also tells us

quickly if we are either riding high, or, maybe, just maybe, getting on at
the end of the line.

Pattern Recognition—Jumping on Board

**Buy on break
above this trendline**

Buy here

**Buy on break
above this trendline**

Buy here

Figure 3. Trendline breaks

There are a number of ways to determine that the stock has completed its retracement and is ready to move. The easiest is to draw a

trendline down across the tops of price bars that make up the retracement. The first day that the stock price closes above that descending trendline is the signal to Buy. (See Figure 3.)

Normal advances consist of *impulsive price moves up* followed by *shallow retracements* followed by *more dynamic rises*. It is a repeating pattern of the best performing stocks. The retracement phase usually covers less then half of the previous advance. When a stock comes back about 25-50% of the preceding advance, (i.e., a move from 10 to 20 is retraced back to 15-17.5), it is time to start looking for the retracement to end. That is the time to buy. How do you know when the retracement is over? The stock stops going down and starts to go up. Sound simple? It *is* simple. (See Figure 4.)

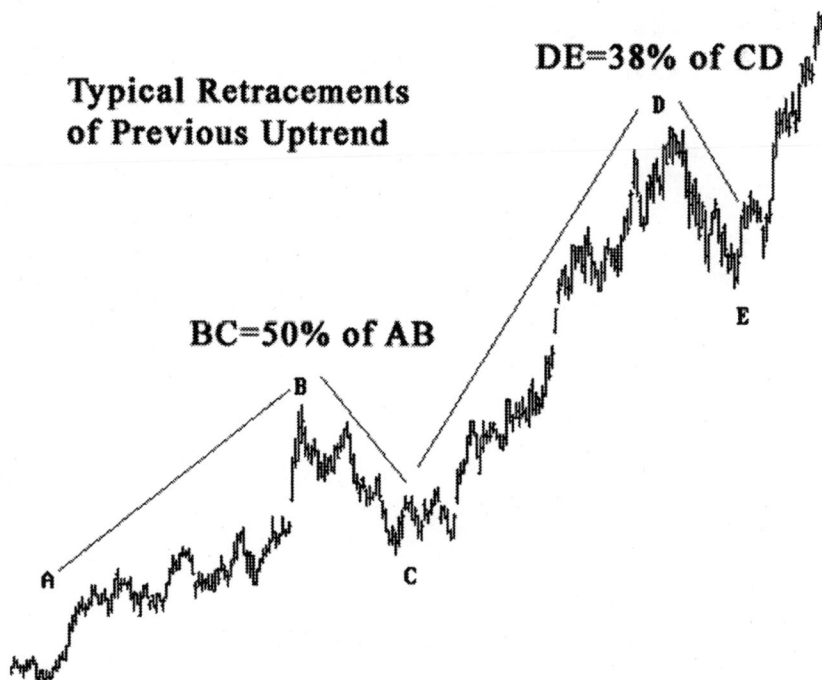

Typical Retracements of Previous Uptrend

DE=38% of CD

BC=50% of AB

Figure 4. Shallow retracements

Pattern Recognition—Oops, going Down

Once you've purchased on the break above the trendline, it's up, up and away...*PROBABLY*. What happens if you're wrong? The stock goes down. Remember that retracement we thought was over? It wasn't, or maybe it wasn't a retracement at all, just the start of a bear market in that stock. Fortunately, our ride down should be short-lived. What we thought was a normal retracement made a low and then started higher. We got on board when it went high enough to convince us the retracement was over. The low point of that retracement should not be taken out, that is to say, the stock should not go much below that low price if indeed this stock is still in an uptrend.

The moment that low is violated, bells and whistles should be ringing all over the place and we sell out. *Period.*

Here's what happened: The stock violated the pattern. It did something it wasn't supposed to do. Sure, maybe it will recover and go on to new highs. But the pattern was violated. We only want to be in stocks that go up. Those stocks exhibit certain bullish patterns. Taking out that retracement low violated the bullish pattern. We're gone. There's other fish in the sea. Other stocks whose patterns are providing better PROBABILITIES of success.

Everything You Always Wanted to Know About Technical Analysis...

In one sentence:

Find stocks that are going up in price and when they exhibit a shallow counter-trend retracement, BUY as soon as that retracement appears to be over.

The ABC's of Technical Analysis

Imagine the box in Figure 5 is the chart of a stock, with the upward sloping diagonal line representing stock prices over a six-month period. Point A is "At-the-beginning" of the upward trend, Point C is the "Conclusion" of the trend, and Point B is where, using the art of technical analysis as previous described, we "*Buy*" the stock. These three points represent the "ABC's" of technical analysis. The object is to find a *Buy* entry point into the stock, as close to "*At-the-beginning*" of the trend, and as far as possible from the *Conclusion* of the trend.

Even if we have identified a stock that is going up, we know nothing about where it is on a continuum of ascending prices. We know the escalator is going up, but we don't know just how much further it has to go. Although it would be wonderful to always get on at A and take the entire ride all the way up to C, it is just more realistic to attempt to get on close to A and off a little past C. What follows is a technique that helps slide that B point down very close to A, and allows for an exit very close to C.

The Essence of Trends

In an effort to 'buy the dips' in uptrending stocks, we perform a trendline analysis, whereby a trendline is drawn down across the tops of price bars that make up the counter-trend downward retracement. The first day that the stock price closes above that descending trendline is the signal to Buy. This use of a trendline can be extrapolated beyond simply identifying the end of counter-trend excursions. Longer, intermediate trends both up and down can be identified simply by connecting the tops of price bars for downtrends and the bottom of price bars for uptrends. As long as prices stay on one side of these trendlines, a trend has been identified and can be easily monitored.

This is an obvious characteristic of trends, that prices keep moving in one general direction. In an uptrend, this means that prices must, by our definition, make progressively higher highs and higher lows. In a downtrend, prices relentlessly make lower highs and lower lows. The trendlines and the progression of prices in a single direction are all there is to know about the trend. (See Figure 6.)

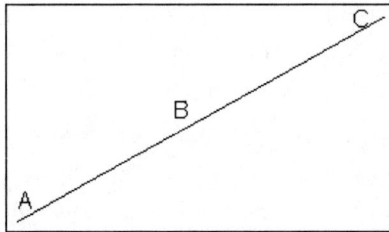

Figure 5. ABC's of technical analysis

Eventually, two things will happen. One, the trend will change. Two, it will become obvious because, (a) prices will breach the trendline, (b) the pattern of higher highs (or lower lows for a downtrend) will end.

Stock prices can only go in one of three directions, *UP, DOWN,* or *SIDEWAYS.*

If prices have been in an extended trend and we see the trendline being broken and the patterns of new highs or new lows end, it is time to anticipate that the old trend is in danger of giving way to a new direction. If a stock that has been making new lows for six months suddenly breaks *up* through the downward-sloping trendline, and starts to make new highs, we can conclude that the downtrend is complete and a new trend, either sideways or up, is about to begin.

Higher Highs = Uptrend

Lower Lows = Downtrend

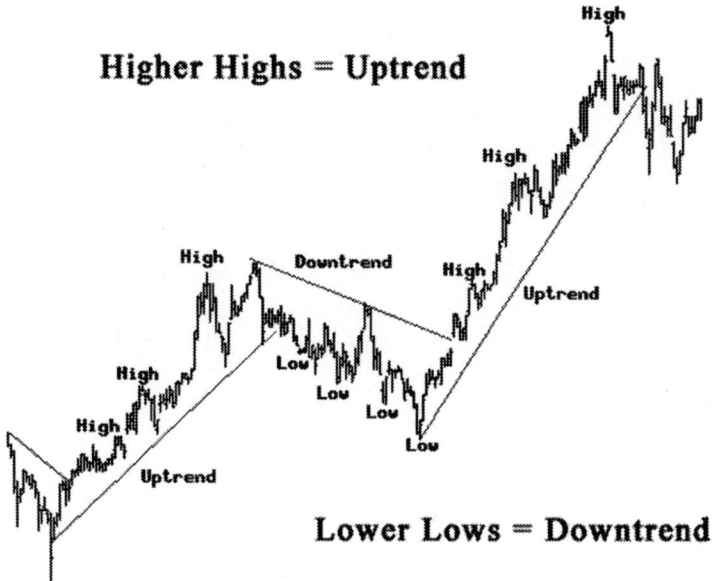

Figure 6. Trendline direction

While a broken trendline indicates the previous downtrend is over, it tells us nothing in and of itself about the ensuing direction of the stock; but, the stock price does. Remember the essence of trends: *In an uptrend, this means prices must, by definition, make progressively higher highs and higher lows. In a downtrend, prices relentlessly make lower highs and lower lows.*

(A) Higher Highs and Higher Lows = UPTREND

(B) Lower Highs and Lower Lows = DOWNTREND

(C) Anything Else = SIDEWAYS

Putting it All Together

1. Entry technique for Buying At-the-Beginning of an *uptrend*:

Buy a stock that has just broken a long downtrend line and begins to make higher highs and higher lows.

2. Exit technique for Selling at the Conclusion of an *uptrend*:

Sell a stock that has just broken a long uptrend line and begins to make lower highs and lower lows.

Insipid Little Details

Concepts presented here describe in very simple and straightforward observations how to identify a trend, how to enter a trend, how to identify a change-in-trend, and how to exit a trend. If it were this easy, why isn't everyone doing it? Because everyone has to complicate matters with insipid little details.

Question:	*How far back do I draw the trendlines? One month, six months, one year, ten years?*
Answer:	*It doesn't matter.*
Question:	*How many new highs does it take to establish a new uptrend?*
Answer:	*It doesn't matter.*
Question:	*How many price bars do I need to start drawing a trendline?*
Answer:	*It doesn't matter.*

Question: *Should I use daily charts, weekly charts, monthly charts or real time intraday charts?*

Answer: ***It doesn't matter.***

Why It Doesn't Matter

The art of technical analysis is the simple matter of observing prices. The techniques presented here provide obvious and easily implemented measurements to aid in that observation. Anything more complicated, more sophisticated, will only work to remove you further from what is really happening to price. Let *the prices* fill in the details for you, otherwise, you will be imposing arbitrary rules, measurements, oscillators, cycles, momentum studies or other artificial parameters upon what is actually unfolding on the charts.

*You will be confused by what the prices **should** be doing, and not observing what prices **are** doing.*

The questions posed above are all good questions. But there are no hard and fast answers other then to realize that if the big picture is clear, the trend, the action of prices around the trendlines, the succession of higher highs or lower lows, then the answers are academic. Whatever time frames you use, however many price bars it takes for you to observe a trend, *that's the answer.*

Find something that works…and use it.

Anatomy of a Trade…Buying and Selling

Figure 7 is ULTK from late 1995 through late 1996. The first and most obvious characteristic of this stock is that it is going UP. Noteworthy is the series of higher highs and higher lows, starting at the lower left hand side of the chart along with the upward-sloping trend-lines that connect the lows of the pattern. The stock provides three series of 'zigs and zags' providing entry opportunities as indicated by the BUY arrows. In each instance, ULTK exhibited a shallow retrace-ment of the prior uptrend and then broke the retracement trendline and resumed it's upward ascent.

Technical Analysis of Ultrak's Price Chart Late June 1996

We are now in this trade, following the uptrend (Figure 8).

Ultrak Chart 6-28-96

1. Stock is going up
2. Retracement of uptrend
3. Breakout buy signal

Figure 7. Price chart Ultrak late 1995 - late 1996

Ultrak July-October, 1996

5 →   6→

4. Uptrend after BUY signal
5. Significant LOW prior to
   new Highs
6. Break of Uptrendline and
   Break of Significant Low

4

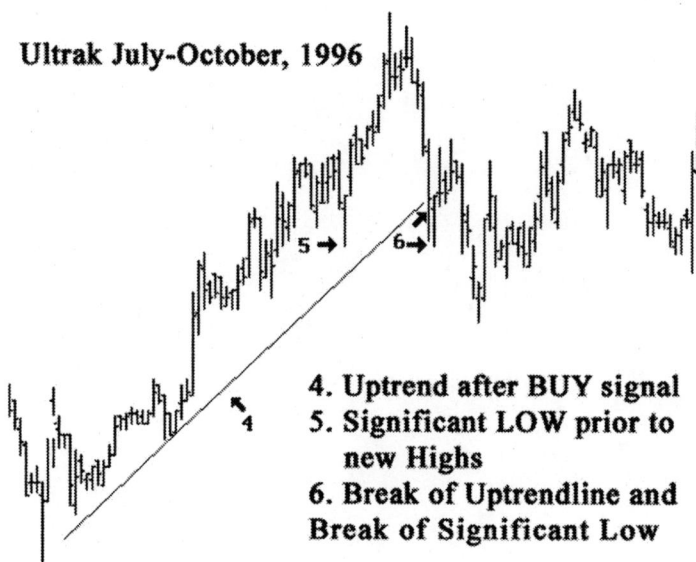

Figure 8. Ultrak uptrend

✓   We first determine that the Major Trend is UP.

✓   We then identify an area of retracement or consolidation.

✓   When that consolidation is over, price's breakout above resistence, a BUY SIGNAL.

This low doesn't take out the up trendline, but we are aware of its significance and would not want to see it taken out. (See Figure 9.)

We see looking at Figure 9 both the up trendline as well as significant low is broken; the stock is no longer going up as it makes lower lows and has broken the uptrend. Time to Exit.

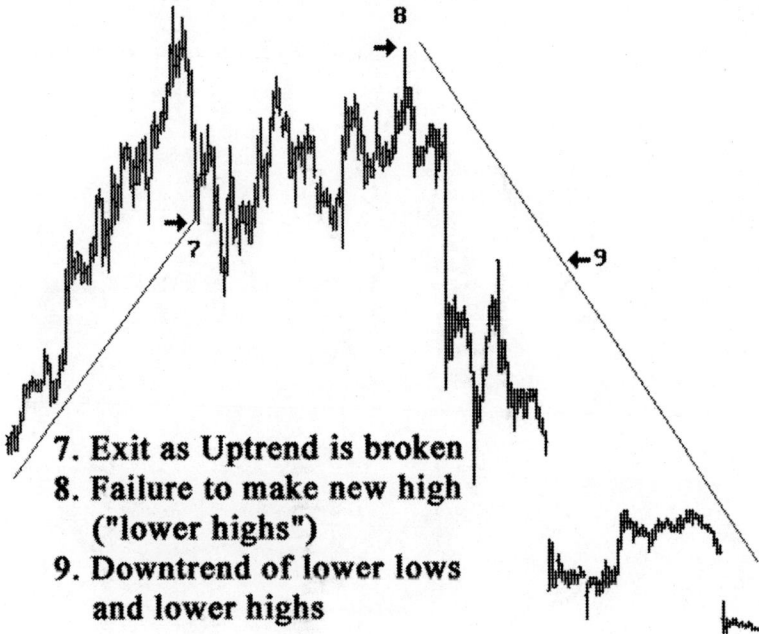

7. Exit as Uptrend is broken
8. Failure to make new high
   ("lower highs")
9. Downtrend of lower lows
   and lower highs

Figure 9. Breakdown

Technical Analysis Lessons from Trendline Breakdown

Reference Exit Point.

✓   Note how stock fails to establish new *uptrend* by making a lower High.

✓ A series of lower lows and lower highs takes back all of the previous gains.

Conclusion

Although there are many rules which seem to surround the mystique of technical analysis, these simple rules will put investors well ahead of the game if they are followed.

Rule # 1. Buy Only Those Stocks That Are Going Up

The trend is your friend when it comes to technical analysis. Why would you want to buy stocks that have an upward pattern? If you are a risk adverse investor, then go with the trend.

Rule # 2. Look for Retracement of Up Trends

Look for those stocks that have exhibited a 25 to 50 percent retracement of previous up trends from their recent highs.

Rule # 3. Be On The Lookout for Obvious Breakout Buy Signals

Look for sudden upward price movements that produce a gap in the price pattern of the stock's chart.

Rule # 4. Know When to Leave The Party (Sell The Stock)

It is time to exit when the stock pattern exhibits a downward trend of lower lows and lower highs.

Chapter 3

What Do Financial Ratios Really Tell You?

By Richard J. Davis, M.D., M.B.A.

...You are now in business school to learn how to perform quantitative analysis using the tools of finance for corporate valuations. Be wary of others' work, their analysis may be wrong! [Excerpt taken from an address given on the first day of class]

-Dr. Sam Richmond, Dean Emeritus
Owen Graduate School of Management
Vanderbilt University

Introduction

This chapter is designed to introduce the reader to the world of fundamental analysis. Although this may seem like a difficult subject to comprehend, this section of the book will give the reader an overview which will help him/her decide what criteria are relevant when assessing companies.

The concept of creating a model and its components for screening stocks will be introduced with a scoring system to quantify this process.

Basics of Surmising A Company's Real Financial Pulse

While in medical school, and later as a resident, I learned how to assess the status of both acutely and chronically ill patients. I learned that conditions producing relatively new or acute events often pose the greatest threat. Trauma, blood loss, or acquired circumstances, such as infection, can tip the balance from good condition to very ill. Rapid intervention was often needed to stabilize the patient and treat the underlying problem. Conversely, changes in those patients with chronic conditions, such as heart problems, hypertension, or diabetes, were often more subtle, and harder to detect. It was more difficult to determine when and what level of intervention was appropriate. The more experienced clinicians were much more adept in detecting a change over time and the need for reduced intervention and treatment. Over time, I acquired those skills, and could readily determine whether someone was acutely ill or had delicate alterations in his/her chronic condition.

Not surprisingly, while in business school, I discovered a set of diagnostic tools that were used to recognize whether a company had good or bad financial health. Similarly, by looking at the financials, I learned to separate the signs and symptoms of those companies struggling or sick from those well and in good health. The healthy companies were often able to grow, expand, and in some cases takeover others by merger and acquisition. My profession has changed, but the diagnostic symptoms of the two disciplines and their systematic approaches have converged.

Cash Flow Analysis…Determining Whether the Corporate Life Blood is Flowing

(Optional Reading)

Although not a part of the Fundamental Model we will discuss later in this book, *cash flow analysis* is an important tool for accomplished investors. Often, investors tend to focus on net income as their sole value gauge, but more experienced investors rely on cash flow which is the money generated by a company from operating activities. In fact, many companies generate more cash flow than net income. This is usually accomplished by a company managing its balance sheet assets or using tax and depreciation treatment to benefit shareholders. Using corporate *cash flow analysis,* investors can discern whether the financial pulse of a company is strong, weak or thready. The following discussion outlines an example where cash flow analysis transcends the usual reported earnings per share and allows the astute investor a tool to identify adverse as well as positive situations facing a company.

I can remember the managerial accounting course where I was introduced to the principles of Largay and Stickney's *Cash Flow Analysis*[2]. (See Table 1.) Professor Germain Böer was one of those superb senior clinicians/professors of accounting who taught me to use strict analytical criteria to evaluate the financial health of a company. As an example, he used W.T. Grant, a notable company up until the mid

---

2 Largay III, J.A., & Stickney, C.P., *Cash Flows, Ratio Analysis and the W.T.Grant Company Bankruptcy. Financial Analysts Journal,* July-August, pp. 51-54.

1970's, to display the importance of strong analysis. The story of W.T. Grant told of profitability and liquidity ratios that were trending downward, but these variables alone did not tell the entire tale. As it turned out, its operations were not generating enough cash, and over time, the burdens of having to borrow money to prop up lagging cash flow placed the company into insolvency. What appeared on the surface to be a healthy company was in fact a struggling corporation which ultimately failed. This was one of my first lessons in the use of analytical models or templates for in depth evaluation of a company's health.

One could ask, could the debacle of W.T. Grant be repeated in today's stock markets? It is unlikely, but possible. Efficient Capital Markets[3] present in the United States are the envy of the world. Companies trading on the stock exchanges must adhere to strict rules of accountancy. Disclosures of corporate financial information often flow at quarterly intervals in the form of earnings reports to analysts in conference calls that disclose the success or failure of the overall corporate strategies and business plan execution. As a result of this efficiency, good and bad news is rapidly reflected in stock prices. Explanations for shortfalls in earnings or earnings exceeding expectations are usually readily available on numerous media sources such as CNBC, Reuters, Dow Jones News Service, Bloomberg and on the Internet. With so many financial analysts looking at specific companies in their area of expertise, the likelihood of adverse cash flow operations being hidden from public knowledge is almost impossible. Both institutional and individual

---

3 Efficient Capital Markets are those where information flows so readily that no investor has knowledge at any point in time ahead of others. The price of the stock reflects any public knowledge reflected in balance sheets, income statements, and dividend announcements.

investors in the market would be informed immediately. This can be illustrated by a more recent example.

In October, 1997, Oxford Health Plans (OXHP) revealed that its new computer systems were having trouble sending out monthly bills to thousands of customer accounts, and were failing to track payments to hospital and physician providers. The same company was heralded for its customer service to patients and positive relationships with providers in providing medical care in a timely fashion. Growth in patient enrollment spurred higher levels of revenue and balance sheet profitability in terms of earnings. The stock soared upward for many years, was a darling of Wall Street, but between late October and early December of 1997, the stock suddenly fell 60%, and plummeted another 15% when the full impact of the problems was disclosed in an analyst conference call. The failure of the new computer systems had caused errors in the collection of over $400 million from customers, and had failed to provide payments of $650 million to providers. The company had a problem. OXHP would go on to *lose* money in the quarter ending December of 1997. Its reported loss of $0.99 versus producing $0.65 in the previous quarterly earnings reports showed investors the magnitude of the problem. In comparison to the story of W.T. Grant, Oxford Health Plan's financial problems were disclosed and fully understood in a few short months rather than several long years and the company survived.

A modern day example where cash flow analysis (See Table 1) can reflect *positive* changes about a company is Federal Express (FDX). Their operating cash flow in the last four fiscal years has been quite robust. In a highly competitive overnight package delivery service, one might ask, how does Federal Express generate cash flow well above its reported earnings per share? Large volume, profitable operations that generate more cash than Federal Express needs in order to cover fixed costs. Operations created $8.71 per share in cash in fiscal year 1997; reported earnings per share were $3.12. Where did the remaining $5.59

go? The company used the cash to finance a net addition of 27 aircraft and 1,600 delivery vehicles. Federal Express is currently using operations yielding excellent cash flow plus debt to increase their distribution network, and expand into new markets.

Annual reports and fiscal year reporting statements are the most readily available sources of information for computing *cash flow analysis.* If you own a company whose share price is falling without explanation or news, especially after an annual reporting period, then using this tool may be useful for you to determine if the company is experiencing poor financial health.

In summary, cash flow analysis can provide the investor with a tool to identify companies whose financial pulse is strong or barely there. With a small amount of practice, calculating cash flow from operations, as seen in Table 1, can provide an important tool to assess a company whose stock price seems truly undervalued. Comparing the company's cash flow to its peers or competitors may provide an insightful lesson for the shrewd investor.

In the next section we will look at *seven principles* all investors should copy and mount on their wall when researching a company.

Table 1. Largay and Stickney's Cash Flow Analysis Model Calculating Cash Flow From Operations

A. Sales or Revenue Sources

- \+ Decrease(-increase) in accounts receivable
- \+ Cash collections on sales
- \+ Other revenues (+ or—adjustments for noncash items)

- = Total Cash collections from operations

B. Cost of Goods Sold (excluding depreciation, amortization, etc.)

+   Increase(-decrease) in inventories
+   Decrease(-increase) in trade payables
+   Operating Expenses
+   Other Expenses (including interest)
+   Increase(-decrease) in prepaid assets
+   Decrease(-increase) in accrued liabilities
+   Income Tax Expense(excluding deferred taxes)
+   Decrease(-increase) in accrued taxes

=   Total Cash from Operations = A—B

C. Net Cash Flows from Operations = A—B

Seven Principles in Diagnosing Healthy Companies...

Over time in B-School (Business School) my physician friends came to call me Stockdoctor™ since I could diagnose a company's health from its financial statement alone without knowing the company's name. It became readily apparent that there were common practices prevalent in discerning healthy companies from ailing ones. The following are characteristics that define healthy companies:

Healthy Companies...

1.   Disclose problems early, fully and with complete candor. Bad news is handled forthrightly without ambiguity. This reflects managerial strength and integrity.

2.   Demonstrate unit volume growth and dollar *growth* in sales. These revenues are real.

3.   Produce *above average* return on assets (ROA)[4], and *increase* return on equity (ROE) over time.

4.   Exhibit financial leverage by having low debt (Low long term debt as a percentage of capitalization). Possess operating leverage by *reducing* fixed and variable costs per unit of goods or services produced over time.

5.   Are profitable companies which show earnings growth with sales, manifest more efficiency and productivity than their competitive peers. (See Chapter 7 on PFT ELS.) Others often have noticed these attributes and are reflected in mutual fund or other institutional ownership.

6.   Are knowledge-based companies that spend money on research and development, whether it is in the form of training of its human capital or innovation for new products and services. Good cash flow is a requisite to fund these endeavors.

7.   Yield sustained earnings, revenue growth to have sufficient assets on the balance sheet to weather economic difficulties such as recessions or competitive pressures in their developing and launching their good(s) or service(s). Key financial ratios, such as *Current Ratio (CR)* which will be defined later, are reflections of this implicit strength.

---

4 ROA or return on assets is defined as a measure of a company's profitability, equal to a fiscal year's earnings divided by its total assets, expressed as a percentage.

Each of these traits are things that I search for in characterizing strong, financially sound companies. When a stock possesses these specific attributes in a quantitative fashion, it is a company that requires further scrutiny and due diligence before being added to my portfolio. *In summary, this is the process behind fundamental analysis and model creation when seeking to find those fundamentally healthy, stable and growing companies.*

The next section discusses some of the controversies that surround fundamental analysis and will attempt to demystify this process for the reader.

Fundamental Analysis Explained—The World Has Changed

Fundamental analysis scrutinizes the myriad of numbers generated about a stock and company and attempts to predict the soundness or weakness of a company in financial terms. The problem is, which numbers are significant barometers of a good or bad investment, and which are not? Often, company CEO's, financial analysts, stock brokers and others discuss terms such as P/E, earnings momentum, or excellent products and markets for the goods or services produced by XYZ company. In the virtual world which we now live in, the fundamentals of companies have taken on a new dimension. In the earlier part of the century, an oil, railroad, shipping, and insurance company all had visible monuments to attest to their fundamental strength as a company. It was easy to judge their success by the number of oil tank cars, freight cars, barges they moved across the country, or how tall the insurance company buildings in major cities stood. Today, most companies have discovered that the bricks and mortar real estate of yesteryear represent high costs to maintain and do not substantially add to the profitability of the company unless they are leasing out most of the building with their name on the cornerstone. An investor can no longer trust these physical manifestations of success to display the true value of a company. He or she must seek out information through many sources such as annual reports, Internet stock research, or business journals. The changes that have taken place over the years have given new importance to these "mere numbers."

An investor must look beyond the name of a company and investigate the real basis for corporate profitability and continued growth. For example, one of the most important factors to consider when examining a company is how well the company is growing and competing both domestically and globally. What decides whether a stock is a good investment or not is how well the company is *doing now* and what it can be expected to do (i.e., grow earnings and become *more* profitable) in the *foreseeable future*. The following are principles which one can use in developing a model for screening stocks which will improve your chances for finding good investments.

Why Do You Need a Fundamental Model?

What many *academicians and financial analysts fail* to realize is that one financial ratio (P/E or price/earnings ratios) is insufficient in determining a company's valuation and underlying financial strength. Call it convention, but don't call it experience or history. A savvy investor realizes that a combination of factors governs the attractiveness of a particular stock. One can quickly learn that a simple approach using a combination of numbers to score a company is a good method to follow. To make things easy to understand and use, it is generally best to have a numerical scoring system where a total of 100 points would be the high score that any company could achieve. How many times have brokers, friends and others recommended a particular stock and gave its P/E as the only compelling reason why *you* should buy the stock? Remember the following.

✔ Key Point:

> No single number or ratio is sufficient to buy a company or stock.

Corollary : *No physician uses a single test or piece of clinical information to make a diagnosis or treat patients.*

How Do We Determine Fundamental Model Scoring ?

So it is in the real world of medicine as it is in business. No solitary ratio or piece of clinical information makes either the diagnosis or the proper assessment of a company. Using multiple criteria with some criteria having greater importance than others, improves the likelihood of a correct diagnosis. If one sees a patient with abdominal pain, tenderness in the right lower quadrant, and elevated white blood cell count, x-rays and other tests will not increase the accuracy of finding an inflamed appendix. Just like investing, in medicine some pieces of clinical information have a greater weighting in the overall ability to make a correct diagnosis.

In assessing companies, there are various components of *growth* and *value* within the Fundamental Model (See Table 1) which have varying degrees of importance. We have assigned different points in order of their significance. Since two major criteria are used for *growth* (earnings growth over five years and the latest 12 months), equal point assignments of twenty-five points have been made. In addition, five different parameters are used to assess *value* in the Fundamental Model. Price/Sales Ratio and Return on Equity (ROE) are considered to be extremely important by knowledgeable investors. The former, Price/Sales Ratio is assigned twenty-five points due to its higher level of importance while ROE is assigned ten points. All other criteria which comprise the value assessment of a company have an equal assignment of five points .

Authors Note:

Balance between growth and value for screening stocks poses a tradeoff between these two broad categories of investing style. It is rare for a company to score points in every category.

Table 1. Fundamental Model Summary Table

Fundamental Model of Stocks you would like to Buy and own....		
Parameter in Model / Archetype	Criteria	Points possible *
% Earning Growth in past 5 years [*earnings growth*]	= or > 25 %	25
Latest 12 mos. EPS Change % (current 12 mos. vs. prior 12 mos.) [*earnings growth*]	= or > 25 %	25
Price / Sales Ratio (P/SR) (*value*)	< or = 1.5	25
Return on Equity (*value*)	= or > 15 %	10
Institutional Ownership (*considered value*)	= or > 30 %	5
Long Term Debt as a % Shareholder's Equity (*value*)	= or < 10 %	5
Current Ratio (*value*)	= or > 2.0	5
Total Points		100

Finding a Passing Score for the Fundamental Model

When a stock is evaluated by the Fundamental Model, and attains a score of seventy-five (75) or greater, it is considered to have passed the fundamental screening. This threshold value of seventy-five comes from looking backwards at stocks with lower scores and determining whether or not they have significant potential price appreciation over time. In fact, those companies whose score equals or exceeds seventy-five (75) seem to perform best. Additional information on determining a passing score can be found in Chapter 4.

Building Blocks of the Model

When assembling a model airplane, you understand that there is going to be more than one piece. In order to have a decent looking model plane, one has to assemble all of the necessary pieces. This concept is also true in developing a financial model for evaluating a stock. I will give you the underpinnings of a model that has been successful over time and its weighting factors or degrees of importance for each component of the model. This model has a balanced weighting of 50% earnings growth, and 50% value, but not all components are equally weighted. This model mirrors decision making strategies used by institutional investors.

In a favorable economic climate, i.e., low interest rates, stable currency, and low inflation, the model has worked well. However, in recessionary times, value, dividends, and lack of price volatility are more important than earnings growth momentum. Therefore the model, depending on various economic conditions, could be weighted differently. Institutional investors would follow a similar strategy and adapt to changing economic conditions.

Model Origins

Some of the concepts of the model are derived from ideas expressed in William O'Neil's *Investor's Business Daily*. Moreover, these concepts are linked with the sound financial principles mentioned in the beginning of this chapter. Specific weights and point assignment are dependent on the value of investors seeking specific types of stock, whether they are growth or value oriented. These concepts provide a precise overview of the specific fundamentals of the company. The investor should use these concepts in deciding whether to be a stock owner.

Model Components—Building Blocks For The Investor

First, and foremost, *earnings growth over the past five years* demonstrates that a company or stock is doing something right. It is becoming incrementally more profitable with increasing revenues or sales while driving down the costs of operation. This in turn increases profitability. This measure of profitability is after taxes, expenses of operation, and production are factored into the overall picture of the company. The company may have multiple product lines or divisions, but it is the *overall picture of net profitability* that produces earnings. The net income, which is the earnings divided by the number of shares outstanding, determines the earnings per share (EPS). *If a company is producing EPS Growth equal to or greater than 25% (EPS >= 25 %) over five years, then that company is assigned 25 points.*

Second, short term *earnings growth over a year's period* is also a critical signal for investors to notice. If a company has produced *significant increased earnings per share growth over the past twelve months (four quarters) versus the twelve months prior to that (prior four quarters), then the company is in the process of building earnings momentum.* This earnings growth is often referred to as Latest 12 mos. EPS Change %. What *are* the pivotal values that build earnings momentum in the short run?

EPS change in the current 12 month periods of 25% greater than the prior twelve month periods is the threshold value of significance and can be considered as a *very* positive sign. Comparing earnings for a year smooths out any extraordinary gains or losses due to seasonality or other factors. Therefore, comparing the *latest* twelve months with the preceding twelve months represents a more accurate picture of the company's strength to *grow* earnings in the short run. Conversely, as one scrutinizes individual quarterly performance, he/she may well find extraordinary quarterly gains due to accounting factors, such as an unexpected gain due to payment of licensing fees, legal settlements, or disposal of assets that would not be otherwise expected. When earnings growth over a year is present, it attracts the attention of mutual fund managers. Ask yourself, which company would you want to own?…One that is sending signals that it is doing something exceeding right among companies in the same industry, or one that is struggling to acquire meager profitability? In fundamental terms, this concept parallels the commentary in Chapter 2 on Technical Analysis to "…buy stocks going up."

Take Home Lesson: If you want to find a winner, pick a stock with a bright light and not the stock with the light that can't be seen on a dark night. (Don't those cars with the super halogen headlights stand apart from the others? Annoying as it is to see them on the road, they certainly catch our attention.)

Money managers and institutions usually want to own only those stocks with the greatest likelihood of price appreciation over time. Consider this rule a positive sign of a company's success. If a company is producing EPS growth in the current 12 month period of 25 % *greater* than the prior twelve month period (Latest 12 mos. EPS Change %) this company has a bright light. In my model, the company is assigned 25 points.

Third, Price/Sales Ratio or (P/S) is another critical determinant associated with the intrinsic value associated with a specific stock. In its simplest terms, it implies the willingness of an investor to pay a dollar in the price of a stock for a dollar in sales. To compute this formula mathematically:

$$\text{P/SR (Price/Sales) Ratio} = \frac{\text{(Price/Share of stock in US\$) (\# of shares outstanding)}}{\text{(Annual Sales or Revenues in US \$)}}$$

Although widely touted as a value tool in academic institutions to determine stocks which are perceived as relatively inexpensive in comparison to their peers, this ratio has gained popularity in James P. O'Shaughnessy's[5] very excellent book. When compared to other single criteria for determining which stocks consistently outperform the S&P 500, this solitary ratio clearly outperformed other financial ratios over a period of 44 years. The critical value for utilizing price to sales ratios is < or = 1.5. *Consequently, if a stock has a P/S equal to or less than 1.5, then the stock is assigned twenty-five (25) points.*

Fourth, return on equity (ROE) is the next part of the model. It is one of the basic factors in determining a company's growth rate of earnings. What does ROE really mean? It is another measure of measuring profitability from a different perspective. Return on assets (ROA) equals earnings *before* income taxes (EBIT)/assets, i.e., [EBIT/assets] of a com-

---

5 O'Shaugnessy, J.P. *What Works on Wall Street: A Guide to the Best-Performing Strategies of All Time:* New York, New York, McGraw Hill,1996.

pany. ROE equals *net profits/equity of the company*. The latter is significantly different since the company's debt to equity, i.e., how much money it owes relative to the value of company, will affect the ROE. Companies with large debt relative to equity add leverage to the capital structure[6]. However, in reality, they must use their earnings before income taxes to pay debt. As a result the company may not have a strong ROE in both the good times as well as the bad times. Therefore companies with low or no debt should possess higher ROA and therefore a higher ROE. *If a company is producing ROE equal to or greater than 15 % (ROE >= 15%), then that company is assigned 10 points.*

Fifth, demand for a growing company's stock must have its heralds and messengers to spread the good word and create activity among the large fund managers. Too much interest in a stock will produce stagnant interest in a company while too little will leave even the best stock or company orphaned for desired ownership. Recalling that some ownership is good, *institutional* ownership or ISH is a must. Brokerage firms recommending the stock to investors should be discounted. Why? Brokerage companies often hold a large number of shares of company stock in their inventory, and in turn, the brokers' representatives are given lucrative incentives to recommend the stock. This is called making a market in a stock and therefore, not considered as part of the institutional ownership spectrum. *A minimum amount of institutional ownership is necessary in the model. Therefore a company having*

---

6 Capital Structure is defined as the mix of the company's different securities comprised of debt and equity. Cash flows assigned to each portion of debt and equity changes the overall value of the company.

institutional ownership greater than 30%, (ISH >= 30%) of the outstanding shares is assigned 5 points.

Sixth, debt is an important factor to review when examining a company's capital structure. There are two types of debt, short term debt (STD) and long term debt (LTD). Of the two, long term debt as a percentage of its overall shareholder's equity (Debt/Equity% or Ratio) is the most critical factor to study. Although traditional finance teaches that increased equity based on the leverage of debt is beneficial to the capital structure[7], one should accept (for the purposes of Chapters 3 and 4) that the lower limits of manageable debt are deemed desirable. Unfortunately, excessive debt severely limits the ability of a company or stock to divert funds to projects or products; instead money is being used to pay off the corporate mortgage. Just as an individual can't buy everything he or she wants because of a house mortgage or car payment, neither can a company. When a highly leveraged company (a company with a lot of debt) needs money to expand, it can either: a) issue more shares, which will dilute earnings; or, b) take on debt at a higher interest rate (corporate bonds) to finance acquisitions or corporate activities. Neither are positive signs. Therefore, it seems reasonable that if a company has huge amounts of debt, it will have difficulty coming up with the necessary capital. In fact, *debt is a curse* since the money needed to repay loans takes away the funds that could have been spent on projects that may prove profitable in the future. *If a company's long term debt relative to it's shareholder's equity is less than 10% (Debt/Equity% or Ratio <= 10 %), assign that stock 5 points.*

Seventh, examining financial solvency is as important as reviewing a company's LTD. Financial solvency is capital necessary to meet short term financial needs or liabilities. The current ratio *or* CR is the ability a company has to meet its current liabilities by liquidating its current assets (turning them into cash). It measures the company's ability to avoid insolvency in times of crisis or where cash repayment of its goods or services (known as accounts receivables) are slowed or delayed. The liquidity provided by the current assets is a critical measure of a company's fundamental strength. Over time, maintenance of a current ratio over 2.0 is a standard universally accepted as an accounting ratio, and is considered as a strong measure of a company's balance sheet. Companies in crisis will have a lower CR, whereas companies with conservative management will often have CR > = 3.0 as a added measure of safety. *If a company's current ratio is greater than or equal to 2.0 (CR >=2.0), then that company earns five (5) points.*

Putting It All Together. Okay I Understand…What's Next ?

Hopefully, by now, using a fundamental analysis model makes good sense. Another frequently asked question: Why use specific weights or scores assigned to each model component? The answer is that some parameters possess more predictive value in identifying individual stocks with the strongest price appreciation potential than others. In addition, when one *uses an optimization model* containing those criteria most used by institutional investors, a 50-50 mix of earnings growth and value factors have been shown to be the most consistent stock out performance.

If we look below at the Fundamental Model, we can see a summary of the specific parameters contained in the model and the threshold criteria and points possible if the model's threshold value is reached. To keep the scoring simple, points attained are either *all* or *none* based on the standards met. Using sliding scales creates too many gray zones of uncertainty in determining whether a specific stock should be awarded points or not. Clear endpoints make the most intuitive sense.

Perhaps the beauty or simplicity in using a scoring model based on 100 points is kin to our own personal experiences in school. We are all familiar with the passing grades in school being above 75 with those in the 70 ranges indicating a traditional C- to D range. If we accept a similar grade for those stocks passing rigorous fundamental valuations, then we have an easy, definable system where the rules of stock owner-ship become simple.

Everything you always wanted to know about fundamental analysis in one sentence:

✔ Key Point:

> *Find and evaluate in depth those stocks whose*
> *scores from the Fundamental Model*
> *yield an aggregate total points of*
> *seventy-five or better. (Model Score >= 75)*

Conclusion

In the next chapter, *Understanding Value Investing*, I will describe in detail the process of performing the individual calculations in each component of the model for our continuing story of Ultrak (ULTK). In addition, a detailed discussion of *value* investing will be undertaken. The use of the fundamental model will be demonstrated in scoring ULTRAK; later we will take an in depth look at the stock's chart to iden-tify buying and selling opportunities.

Chapter 4

Understanding Value Stock Investing

By Richard J. Davis, M.D., M.B.A.

Put your confidence in us, give us your faith and your blessing and under Providence all will be well. We shall not fail or falter, we shall not weaken or tire. Neither the sudden shock of battle nor the long drawn trials of vigilance or exertion will wear us down, give us the tools and we will finish the job.

-Winston Churchill, Prime Minister of England during World War II

Introduction

Personal development as an investor comes with constant learning, challenging the *status quo*, and exploring new ideas and frontiers. If the future always replicated the past, then investing and making money in stocks would be easy. It does not. You have to educate yourself, feel comfortable with the jargon, terminology and pitfalls behind any source of measurement that attempts to define a stock you are researching.

Okay, it is time to take a break if you have been reading this book from Chapter 1. Get a cup of coffee, soft drink or your favorite beverage before reading this chapter. Why, you ask? Well, this one is going to be heady. You will be taking an in depth journey into understanding and interpreting fundamental analysis. I will attempt to explain fundamental analysis in an easy to read fashion. Afterwards you will be able to discuss these concepts with your spouse, friends or colleagues. Instead of pursuing hot tips at cocktail parties or other social events, you will instead have the opportunity to demonstrate *your knowledge* about the current stock or company of interest that you are researching by discussing a company's key ratios such as its high return on equity (ROE) rather than simply its unique story for delivery of a product or service in the marketplace. Admittedly, however, a good story always sells since it is the lowest common denominator in our vocabulary of investing. Unfortunately, good stories do not always make good companies to buy into as partial owners in the form of stock shares.

All investors possess the dream of finding winning stocks that will ultimately make money rather than watching a stock falter downward after purchase. Finding stocks on your own rather than relying on the advice of friends, family, or broker is the ultimate goal of investors who wish to develop a stock research methodology. Therefore, using the fundamental model alluded to in Chapter 3 is just one facet of performing your own due diligence before making the rational decision to purchase a stock. A by-product of these lessons will be the creation of a savvy, self-confident investor with a disciplined approach toward investing.

This chapter will discuss classic value investing and make the transition to the concept of using an investment model. In the subsequent chapter, I will tackle an *in depth* discussion of fundamental stock analysis and how to score a stock using the authors' current Fundamental

Model. Also, I will take you on a tour of our web-based Fundamental Calculators. These calculators will simplify the complex financial functions necessary to comprehend growth for earnings and start the reader with the building blocks of stock screening discussed in Chapter 9 later in the book.

To gain a better understanding of fundamental analysis, each parameter of the *Fundamental Model* will be explained in greater detail than the previous chapter. The wisdom behind each criterion will be explained in common sense terms. Each concept, with its respective formula, will be explained and utilized through lessons. With the calculations readily derived from reliable sources of information, the reader will gain self-confidence in their comprehension of the individual tools used for identifying fundamentally sound stocks. Carrying forward on our initial story about Ultrak from Chapter 1, we will illustrate the application of practical fundamental and technical analysis.

Modeling Origins

To gain mastery or understanding of a field of study, one has to be immersed in the waters or flood of ideas before real insight takes hold. Andrew Lloyd Webber played with models of Shakespearean theaters and began in his mind to write music and stage plays of tremendous beauty and elegance. Taking a real idea from T.S. Elliot's *Old Possum's Book of Poems*, he imagined and created the smash Broadway Musical, *Cats*. Similarly, Frank Lloyd Wright, famous architect of the twentieth century, was given a set of geometric wooden blocks called Froebel blocks by his grandfather as a child. When once asked how they influenced his life, he replied, "*...the maple wood blocks...are in my fingers to this day* "- (Frank Lloyd Wright, *age 88*.) Both men were influenced by their environment to create endearing music, theater, architecture, and visual beauty. Each of us are influenced by events and people in our past and these influences will shape our destiny and influence our knowledge. As humans, we subscribe subtlety to chaos[8] and systems theories without ever realizing it. Although not as dynamic as the highly acclaimed Webber and Wright, I would like to share with you my story on what formalized fundamental modeling for me.

In the Beginning…My First Career

In medical school, the traditional models for instruction were patients with illnesses and diseases. We would often gather in or near the patients' rooms to discuss the patients' conditions and review what the patients had said about their diseases or illnesses and how it affected their life. Afterwards, the patients' X-Rays and pathology slides were reviewed and we listened carefully to our professors talk about human disease, diagnosis, and treatment options. At that time, I could not have predicted twelve years later I would be in business school. Once again, the learning process was similar. The main difference was that now I was studying companies instead of patients. Some companies were sick, while others were healthy and profitable. My tools had changed from stethoscopes, x-rays and lab tests, to financial calculators, spreadsheets, and computers.

In keeping with our promise to educate the investor about the basics of fundamental and technical analysis, we will use Ultrak for continuity. Using Ultrak will illustrate the principles of researching a company for key fundamental information. This can easily be done for any company

---

8 Chaos Theory is a branch of mathematics that holds that what appears to be chaos or disarray holds repetitive patterns if we but look closely for them.

or stock. As you know, the universe of companies and stocks is quite large. In a single day, you might encounter 100+ companies or products and wonder whether or not they are good companies to own a part of through their stock. Fundamental analysis, model screening and ultimately stock screening coupled with technical analysis tenets, will afford the reader another tool in his or her tool box. These tools will enhance the reader's ability to analyze companies or stock before purchasing and re-evaluate their health during ownership.

Fundamental Stock Analysis—Growth or Value?

Investors have always been torn between selecting a stock based on either *growth* or *value*. Clearly, both sides say their methodology is the best strategy to follow in finding stocks that perform well over time against the common benchmark of the S&P 500. Like yin and yang, growth and value retain the character of two separate but interconnected systems. In down markets such as those in 2000 and 2001, technology stocks with relatively high P/E ratios were mercilessly sold off due to their failing to produce *earnings visibility*[9].

Companies that are growth oriented show tremendous earnings growth over time. Sometimes their growth pattern appears parabolic (i.e., almost straight upwards) when charted over time, reaching upwards towards the stratosphere. Traditional valuation for companies, consisting of the price of the stock divided by its earnings or P/E, often

---

9 Earnings visibility can be loosely translated by growth companies CFO's (Chief Financial Officer) as stating "…we will no longer be able to maintain double and triple eps growth looking forward into the next quarter or beyond."

exceeds the S&P 500 market multiple[10]. Unfortunately, these factors can make certain stocks appear to the average investor as very risky. In fact, when one looks carefully at these companies price patterns over time, tremendous upward and downward volatility is often commonplace. Should the average investor shun these companies? After all, many of these stock prices double or triple over a relatively short period of time despite the price volatility. As my barber asked me in early summer 2001, "...*is it time to buy Cisco now since the price is so low?*" The answer to that question will be explained in the next chapter on earnings growth and *momentum*.

Value Investing...Less Price Volatility

On the other hand, if you follow the value investing strategy of Graham and Dodd[11], then ownership of momentum stocks makes little sense when based on traditional determinants such as P/E. Without steady earnings over time, purchasing any of these stocks would be considered taboo since their P/E ratios would be deemed too high above the market multiple P/E. Graham's approach to determining intrinsic value focuses on the company's tangible assets, earnings dividends, and financial strength.

Graham defines two categories of investors: *defensive* investors, and *enterprising* or *aggressive* investors. According to Graham, *defensive* investors should only own stocks of important companies with a strong

---

10 Market multiple consists of taking aggregate earnings per share of the S&P 500 stocks, and dividing by the current S&P 500 Value. Historical average S&P 500 market multiple from 1950-present is 14 with a standard deviation of four; range is 7-23.

11 Refers to the Classical Treatise on Value Investing, by Benjamin Graham, called *The Intelligent Investor*, continually published since 1934.

financial base and long history of profitability. Graham defines *enterprising investors* as those who attempt to screen companies in hopes of finding those with strong value. For the *enterprising* investor, the intelligent effort expended in analyzing stocks should be rewarded. For the novice, this type of valuation is difficult to comprehend and replicate for each company without an extraordinary investment of time. Table 1 outlines the enterprising investor's criteria for stock screening. To simplify this process, the reader can follow the easy-to-follow steps contained in Figure 1. This will allow the reader to implement a rapid value analysis of their stock in question. How well does your stock fulfill Graham and Dodd's *intelligent investor* category?

Table 1 . Value Investing Criteria of Intelligent Investors

Graham's Value Investing Parameters	Criteria
Low Price / Earnings Multiple	P/E values in lower 10 % of all stocks
Financial Condition	Long term debt < 110 % of current assets
Earning Stability	Positive earnings over past 5 years
Dividend Policy	Company must have some dividend for shareholders
Earnings Growth	Earnings growth in last year must be higher than 5 years ago
Price / Book Ratio or P/B[12]	Less than or equal to 120 % of tangible book value

12 Price to book ratio or P/B is the current share price divided by its book value. Book value assumes sale of the company and all its assets.

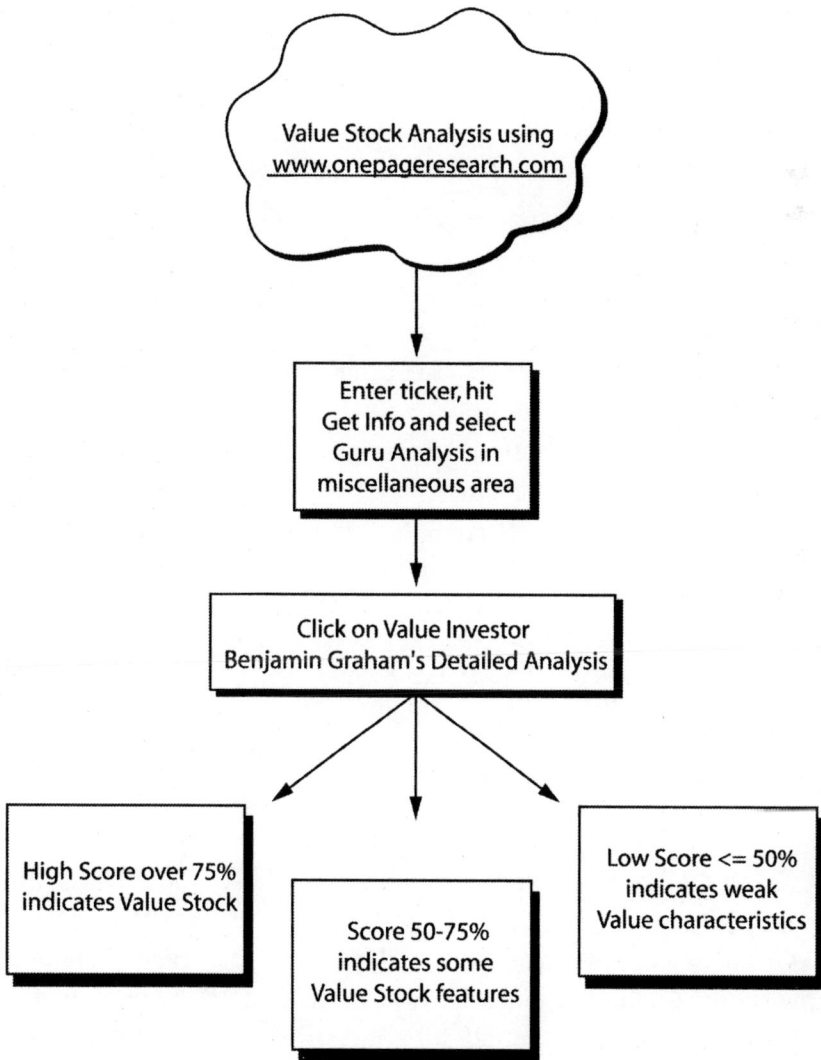

Figure 1. Value Stock Analysis

Warren Buffett, Another Famous Value Investor Who Likes Value with Growth

In summary, current value investors such as Warren Buffett[13] integrates the traditional value principles described. *Value investors simply wait for the market to recognize these undervalued stocks which will in turn drive their share price higher.* The time frame for this recognition may be years rather than weeks or months. For example, when Buffett identifies an undervalued company, then one of two events occurs: Either a large number of shares are purchased, or a company is acquired as what happened in the summer of 1997 when he bought International Dairy Queen. Warren Buffett's strategy requires positive earnings in each of the last five years. This is the type of growth he expects and seeks. More about using Warren Buffet's strategy in Chapter 10, *One Page Research—Probing a Company*.

As you evaluate researched stocks you are investigating and come across one with equivocal value investing characteristics (a score = > 50 but = < 75 %) using the One Page Research Guru Analysis section of the site, it is quite easy to add either to a shadow portfolio or your watch list. Revisiting the stock every three to six months should be appropriate.

Fundamental Model Scoring System

With these concepts of value investing in mind, using the traditional approach of Graham's, *"Intelligent Investor"*, our Fundamental Model relies both on *value* and *growth* for choosing a stock. This is an attempt to strike a balance between the two disciplines by using an equal weighting between value *and* momentum. *The Fundamental Model*

---

13 Readers are directed to: Robert Hagstrom, Jr., *The Warren Buffet Way*. New York, New York: John Wiley & Sons, Inc.,1995.

builds a bridge that integrates the diversity and strengths of the two strate-gies while reducing the risk of allowing one technique to dominate. Finding stocks that fulfill *both* criteria should produce a list of stocks that will be *head and shoulders* above their peers. Since these selected stocks possess characteristics of both investment strategies, they should possess potential for superior price performance. Creating an easy to use Fundamental Model based on value and momentum parameters has worked well in the past and should greatly assist the *enterprising investor* who uses our Fundamental Model characteristics to screen stocks for further investigation and study.

Recognizing that the various components of *growth* and *value* within the Fundamental Model (See Table 2. Fundamental Model Summary) have varying degrees of importance, we have assigned different points in order of their significance. Since two major criteria are used for *growth*, equal point assignments of twenty-five (25) points have been made. On the other hand, five different parameters are used to assess *value* aspects of the Fundamental Model. One parameter, Return on Equity (ROE), is considered to be extremely important by experienced investors such as Warren Buffett. Therefore, ROE has a greater level of importance and is assigned ten (10) points. All other criteria which comprise the value assessment of a company have an equal assignment of five (5) points.

What is a Passing Score ?

When a stock is evaluated by the fundamental model and obtains a score of seventy-five (75) or greater, it is considered to have passed the fundamental screen. Those stocks whose scores are less than seventy-five should be revisited in the future. However, to identify strong stocks in the present, we need to investigate only those which have a passing score. *All* or *none* scoring is employed for the Fundamental Model point assignments thus allowing for some companies to gain a passing score of seventy-five (75) points without having to pass all criteria as seen in Graham's classical approach of value investing.

Over time, the financial markets can change. Should valuation of stocks favor value factors over earnings growth or vice versa, then the model can adapt and change its weighting of individual parameters. Evolution of these changes can be subtle, but realignment of the Fundamental Model should continue to focus the individual in the direction of finding those stocks or companies whose stock prices trend upward over time. No system known to fundamental stock analysis is perfect, but fundamental screening of stocks will continue to provide the tools for the individual investor to be self-reliant and confident in his/her judgement while reducing the universe of over 8,000 stocks to a more manageable number which can be more throughly investigated.

Table 2. Fundamental Model Summary Table

Fundamental Model of Stocks you would like to Buy and own...		
Parameter in Model / Archetype	Criteria	Points possible
% Earning Growth in past 5 years [*earnings growth*]	= or > 25 %	25
Latest 12 mos. EPS Change % (current 12 mos. vs. prior 12 mos.) [*earnings growth*]	= or > 25 %	25
Price / Sales Ratio (P/SR) (*value*)	< or = 1.5	25
Return on Equity (*value*)	= or > 15 %	10
Institutional Ownership (*considered value*)	= or > 30 %	5
Long Term Debt as a % Shareholder's Equity (*value*)	= or < 10 %	5
Current Ratio (*value*)	= or > 2.0	5
Total Points		100

Conclusion

First, do you see any familiarity to Graham's guidelines for the *Intelligent Investor* and the characteristics of my fundamental model? Second, ask yourself, which of these two models possesses an almost intuitive feel or ease of use? Third, if you could screen stocks for each of these variables easily on the Internet, would this save you time? Fourth, and lastly, if the answer to most of these questions is *yes*, then you are well on your way to understanding Confirmatory Analysis.

Chapter 5

Understanding Growth Stock Investing

By Richard J. Davis, M.D., M.B.A.

Tell me and I forget,
Teach me and I remember,
Involve me and I learn.

-Chinese proverb

Introduction

The Chinese proverb that opens this chapter may be one of the most truthful statements on the art of learning that has ever been made. Everyone has at one time or another sat in a classroom, listened to a didactic lecture, and really wondered if they were doing anything more than listening. When queried by our parents, " *what did you learn in school today?*" Our response would be similar to my children's when asked this same question,"...*Oh, the usual, nothing special.*" By failing to involve ourselves in the matrix of information, we are put at a distance from information rather than really learning anything. Science experiments in high schools across the country display age-old chemical processes not because we need to make sure that an acid can still equalize the pH of a base, but to involve the students in the scientific process instead of just lecturing about it. Without this sort of interaction, what we find happening is that more and more people develop *Information Anxiety*[14] about a particular subject. Investigating Growth investing is one of these subjects for most people. Hopefully after reading this chapter, you will be able to interact with information about stocks, and gain a bit of knowledge about investing concepts related to the term *growth* (in terms of EPS and REV or Sales). Admittedly, the concept is complex, but I will attempt to walk you through the process, step by step.

The Fundamental Model in Seven Easy Steps

Step 1: Earnings Growth Over the Past 5 years—Momentum Indicator

Earnings growth over time has long been an indicator of high-performing stocks. Like a ball rolling down a hill, earnings gather speed. Accelerating earnings create a sense of desirability for ownership by institutional and individual investors alike. The term momentum is a

---

14 Saul Wurman, *Information Anxiety 2*. Indianapolis, Indiana: Que Publishers, 2000. *Information Anxiety* is produced by the ever-widening gap between what we understand and what we think we should understand. Information Anxiety is the black hole between data and knowledge. It happens when information doesn't tell us what we want to know.

logical connotation for this phenomenon of stock price appreciation that correlates with increasing earnings growth over time.

Characteristics of pure momentum investing:

✓   *Searching for stocks with unsustainable earnings per share growth rates of 20-25 % into the foreseeable future.*

✓   *Looking for companies with huge profit margins over their competitors.*

✓   *Companies with new product introductions that fuel the potential growth of earnings.*

✓   *Using no other parameters of stock selection other than earning growth.*

Looked at it another way, earnings growth relies exclusively on the business's tempo. When the growth rate falls, the stock price can collapse without news, or for other reasons that would explain a precipitous fall in the stock price. Stocks with extraordinary Price/Earnings or P/E's multiples equal to or greater than 50 often fall into the category of stocks for which momentum players will pay ever-increasing prices. This is what was seen in the beginning of March 2000 and lasting to the summer of 2001 during the so-called Internet boom. *Inability to forecast revenues leads to a failure in earnings visibility.* These were the buzzwords for many companies either pre-announcing or reporting shortfalls in quarterly earnings as companies repeatedly used the same language to describe a profit recession in Corporate America. What were these great American companies really saying and what did it really mean? In my vocabulary, the translation was simple. Our business has fallen off the cliff and we can't see the other side!

Momentum players or institutional investors in high *growth* companies often fail to disclose their exit strategy or announce the sale of their stock as they take profits. Such warning often comes to individual investors too late, as impending doom to corporate profits occurs and the stock price diminishes rapidly or *gaps down*. Institutional investors, or those with large holdings, have historically learned of such information long before the news was reported in the financial press. With the passage of the SEC's *Selective Disclosure Rule* in late 2000, the playing field was leveled between institutional and individual investors. More about this later in Chapter 10.

The main pitfall of pure momentum investing is buying other people's forecasts (Wall Street sell-side analysts) that may or may not come to fruition. If you are following a momentum investor's lead, then watch your stock carefully and be prepared to sell by using a predetermined stop/loss order[15].

Since momentum *does* have its place in choosing outstanding stocks, we need to understand the subtleties of momentum before proceeding further. If we reach back to physics classes in our past and remember the equation for Momentum:

$$p \text{ (momentum)} = M \text{ (Mass)} \times V \text{(Velocity)}$$

Then we can use that as an analogy to help us understand momentum investing jargon. We could also say that:

Momentum = Growth in Earnings Accelerating over time

---

15 Stop/loss order refers to the practice whereby an order is placed for the sale of a stock if the price falls to that level. Used for stocks with volatile price action to protect profits gained.

To better illustrate momentum, consider the sinking of the H.M.S. Titanic. The infamous ship was traveling at 22 knots, and weighed 46,000 tons when it hit the iceberg. Using the momentum formula, this translates into 1,102,000 tons*knots of momentum directly into the path of the iceberg! No wonder the unsinkable ship did not survive. (See Figure 1.)

Figure 1. H.M.S. Titanic

Momentum is a vector quantity, and in that sense, it is dependent on direction. In the same way as the Titanic continued moving in the same direction as it plowed through that fateful iceberg, a stock exhibiting strong earnings momentum will continue to rise in price as long as the momentum stays strong...and as long as it doesn't hit an iceberg (failure in earnings growth). The term earnings growth has its origins in finance where the interest of capital investment or net income generated through appreciation is constantly reinvested in the company. Companies with significant earnings growth forego dividends to shareholders and reinvest their profits back into the company, using these profits to expand the business. *Stocks with high earnings growth often pay no dividends to shareholders. Rewards of ownership are often paid in stock splits or price appreciated stock.* Why do they do this rather than pay regularly scheduled dividends of cash to shareholders? The explanation is founded in the current tax policy of the United States. Company's paying dividends are taxed to the individuals as ordinary income. These dividends are considered double taxation since the corporation already pays taxes on net income or earnings. When a portion of net income is passed to individuals in the form of dividends, it is taxed again. Hence the term double taxation for corporations who pay cash dividends to shareholders. On the other hand, capital appreciation of a stock that does not pay dividends is taxed only when the security is sold. If a stock is held for a period of 18 months, its tax rate is based on long term capital gains. Which is better for the individual stockholder, a company paying dividends, or one whose growth is fueled by its own internal cash generation system? In simple terms, it depends on the mind set and age of the individual and whether he/she makes investment decisions based on value or growth.

Returning to our example of Ultrak and its earning's growth over five years, let's look at which of the following tells the story of success better, *a change in earnings over time vs. the degree of earnings growth over the same five year period.* Take a look at Ultrak's *EPS (earnings per share)* graph in Figure 2.

Ultrak Inc. (ULTK)

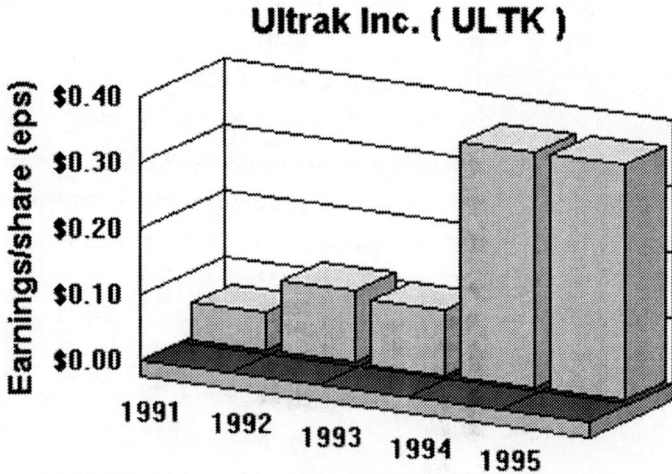

Figure 2. Ultrak EPS 1991-1995

Perhaps your first question might be what is the *definitive change* in earnings from FY 1991-1995?

$$\text{Five year Change in Earnings} = \frac{\text{FY 1995 EPS—FY 1991 EPS}}{\text{FY 1991 EPS}}$$

$$\text{Five year Change in Earnings} = \frac{\$0.36—\$0.06}{\$0.06} = \frac{\$0.30}{\$0.06}$$

Five year Change in Earnings = *500% change in earnings*

Does this imply that the company expanded its business five-fold to attain this degree of profitability? Perhaps it sold assets from the balance sheets or specific business segments to achieve this sensational change in earning. Lastly, did Ultrak intrinsically grow the business by a factor of over five-fold? These are difficult questions to answer by simply looking at the above two sets of earning numbers in 1991 and 1995. (Figure 2) does not answer this question any more clearly.

Now let's take a look from another perspective and try explaining how a change in earnings effects growth. We might phrase the question differently. *What is the rate of sustained growth over five years necessary to grow earnings per share from $0.06 to $ 0.36?* If you reexamine Ultrak's EPS Growth, then you will see *clearly defined earnings* growing slowly *over time and producing momentum.* This is the main reason why graphically depicting earnings is a much better visual learning experience than looking at two isolated numbers which represent events five years apart. [Remember the earlier story of identifying stocks whose chart patterns show *upward price movement?*] Momentum is one of the major ingredients favored by institutional investors and individuals who desire companies which foster rapid stock price appreciation.

Personally, I always understand these concepts better if they are depicted in a graphical format. One quick way to see EPS growth for any stock is to use *www.onepagereserarch.com.* Figure 3 leads the reader through simple steps to create a rapid diagram that graphically represents EPS growth for any stock.

Understanding Growth in Finance Terms

Having first visualized EPS Growth graphically, we are now ready to explain the concept of simple interest growth versus simply a change in earnings over five years. In companies where all the profits are reinvested in the company, no dividends are paid. Accordingly the investor's individual shares of profits per share are reinvested in the company for *future* growth.

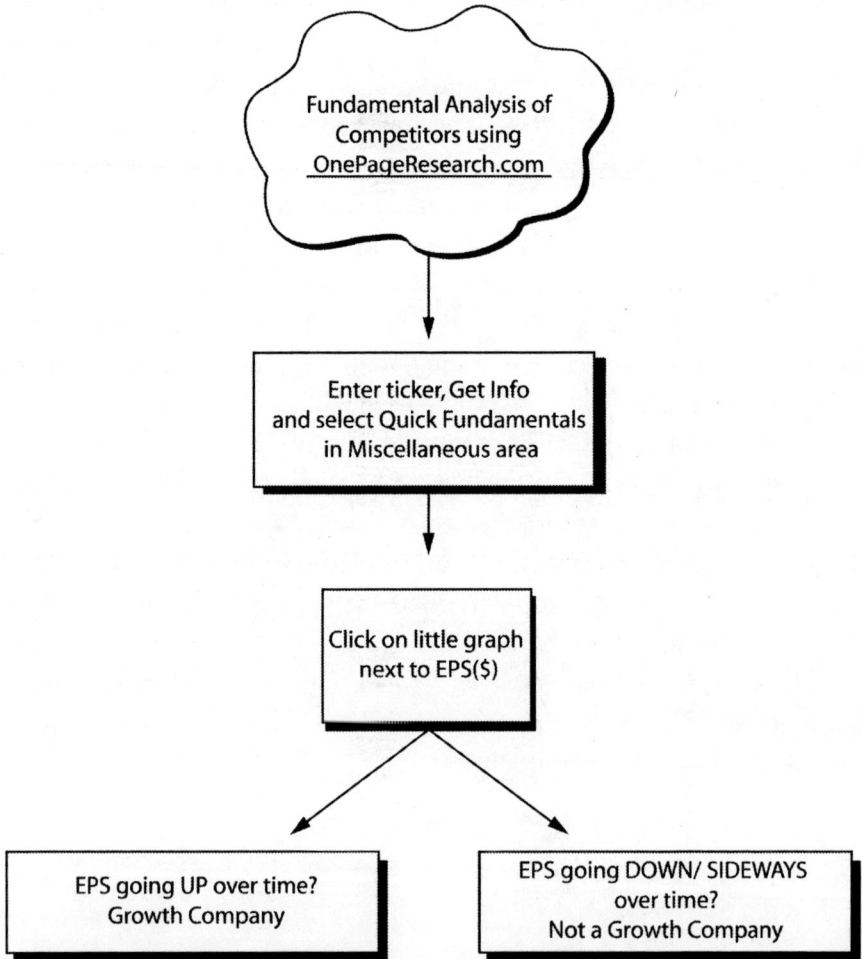

Figure 3. Graphical EPS depiction

To calculate the compounding nature of these profits over time in terms of how the business is actually growing, we must use a finance calculator because the formulas require performing exponential functions (See formula below). In our case, we are observing earnings per share over the previous five years, and we are trying to determine the company's inherent *growth* rate of those earnings. This simple finance formula is the basis for many computations in the finance and banking industry used to compute annuity and leasing computations. In our example, the value of the most recent earnings per share (EPS) by convention is called future value or FV. Earnings per share (EPS) which occurred five years ago are termed present value or PV. We want to know the rate at which those earnings have grown over five years to achieve earnings per share (EPS) now.

$$\text{Future Value} = \text{Present Value}\ (\ 1+r\ )^t$$

Where Future Value (FV) = **EPS** in year 5 or 1995 (in our case $ 0.36)
Present Value (PV) = **EPS** in year 1 or 1991 (in our case $0.06)
t is the period in years = 5 (for years 1991-1995)
r is the rate of *growth over the period t* of five years

Solving,

$$0.36 = 0.06(1+r)^5 \qquad *$$

$r = 0.43$ or 43 %

* My solar calculator won't solve this one, but my HP-12C does!

Fundamental Model's Use of Earnings Growth Over Past Five Years

By now, you have acquired some understanding of the basics of finance and understand why earnings growth over five years is so important. *Assessing the real growth rate of a company's earnings is more important than the assessing its rate of change. Strong growth suggests a company with strong underlying fundamental strength.* Such stellar earnings growth attracts not only *institutional* but individual investors as well. Unfortunately, extremely high rates of earnings growth are difficult to sustain over a long term period. Entry of competitors in similar markets with superior products often drives customers to alternative solutions, thus, adversely affecting the high profit margins necessary to produce high earnings per share. Searching for companies growing over 15-20% annual EPS Growth yields a portfolio of null stocks. Alternatively, in mid-2000 to 2001, an overall slowdown in demand forced many technology companies with double digit EPS growth to fall to single digit EPS growth, and in some cases, negative EPS growth. Such events in the macroeconomic environment are impossible to predict, but such drastic downturns created many investors who saw their often once loved stocks fall to significantly lower levels.

Let's consider the concept of PEG Ratio or a P/E ratio divided by EPS growth for any given period. If a company has *decreasing* EPS growth, then the denominator of this ratio is also decreasing and the resultant PEG Ratio exceeds one. Attractive valuations for growth companies are often when PEG is less than one or PEG < 1. Unfortunately, when growth companies lose their growth, their attractiveness wanes and institutions and individuals may sell them from their portfolios unless they believe the downturn in growth is temporary. It may take some time for these companies to return to previously high levels of growth once they have lost their momentum.

If you are not inclined to perform these financial calculations, then 5-Yr EPS Growth is readily available using One Page Research and following the simple instructions in Figure 5.

On the other hand, if you are like me and wish to know how to perform these calculations, then the optional reading section will cover the subject in greater detail.

In our Fundamental Model, those stocks whose 5-Yr EPS growth is *equal* to or greater than 25% are assigned 25 points.

Using the Web Based Financial Calculator

(Optional Reading)

The following section is designed for the reader who wishes to have a better understanding of the mathematical derivations for determining *earnings growth over the past five years*. The lay reader can simply skip to the next section without losing any of the important concepts contained in this chapter.

An easier technique used to perform earnings growth over five year calculations is to use our web site at *www.confirmatoryanalysis.com*. Using the Fundamental Model Calculator-Advanced, you will be prompted for the values of EPS in the first year [Year 1] (corresponding to the PV in our example above) and EPS [Year 5] is EPS in the current fiscal year (corresponding to FV in the example above). Inputting these values plus other fundamental criteria in the Fundamental Model will generate a score based on a company's underlying financial ratios which can be used to assess the strength of that company or stock.

From our example above, the Fundamental Model Calculator-Advanced would appear as it does in Figure 4. Input the other data found on the web and you will produce a fundamental score for any stock with our weighting and point scoring system.

Figure 4. Fundamental Model Calculator-Advanced on line

[Fundamental Model Calculator Page]

Name of Stock or Ticker: __Ultk__

Earnings/Share (eps) in Year 1
(Current Fiscal Year *minus* 5 years ago) __0.06__

Earnings/Share (eps) in Year 5
(Current Fiscal Year)   __0.36__

Earnings Growth in Last 12 mos.
(Enter # as Percent)
Price to Sales Ratio (PS/R or P/S)
(Use two decimal places)   _____

Return on Equity (ROE)
(Enter # as percent)   _____

Institutional Holdings % (ISH)
(Enter # as percent)   _____

Long Term Debt as a % of
Equity   _____

Current Ratio (CR)   _____

Total Points   (100 possible)   _____

Step 2: Earnings per Share (EPS) Growth in Latest Twelve Months— Creating a Measure of Short-Term Growth

The next step is to understand the role of short-term *growth*. Admittedly, there are many variations on this theme using EPS growth in the past fiscal year, TTM (Trailing Twelve Months) or in EPS Change in the Latest 12 months. Latest 12 mos. EPS Change is readily found on many financial web sites. If you recall, earning growth over five years was a measure of long term *growth* of the company. Institutional investors, portfolio managers, and analysts look for companies that are really executing their corporate business plan and competitive strategies[16] well in both the past twelve months, and past five years as well. If you have ever listened to CNBC and watched stock commentators analyze quarterly earnings, then you are familiar with the impact of changes over the prior twelve months in earnings. Stock prices can literally fall from the sky or soar to the heavens based on earnings announcements. For this reason, many financial analysts spend countless hours attempting to forecast earnings.

Interestingly, when earnings estimate *shortfalls* occur, excuses are plentiful. Commonly heard excuses may include one or more of the following:

✓ Loss of sales in the past quarter
✓ Lower profit margins due to pricing pressures
✓ Currency fluctuations

---

16 Competitive Strategy denotes a niche or an opportunity that a company follows among its peers to gain or maintain a strategic position in the marketplace. The following is considered the best work in understanding corporate strategy. Michael M. Porter, *Competitive Strategy: Techniques for Analyzing Industries and Competitors*: New York, New York: Free Press, 1989.

✓ Taking charges against earnings for events such as providing early retirement or layoffs for employees (often called restructuring)

Miscellaneous seasonality factors and unpredictable events are often to blame for missed numbers[17]. A simple example of this seasonality might be the failure of quarterly earnings estimates for a gas pipeline supply company due to weak demand for their products in a warm winter such was experienced in the El Nino winter of 1997-1998.

Conversely, when earnings expectations *exceed* even the whisper number[18] of earning projections, stocks may move higher due to the earnings surpassing even the best case scenario projections of growth in earnings. Companies have to announce how well or poorly they are doing, quarter after quarter. Ultimately, the stock is constantly being revalued and either the shares are being accumulated (bought) or distributed (sold).

✔ Key Point:

If we observe sequentially the last four quarters of earnings per share growth and compare it to the previous twelve month period, blips in earnings are smoothed out and a more meaningful interpretation about a company's short term earnings growth is generated.

Remember, using the Latest 12 mos. EPS Change or 1-Yr EPS Growth is a more predictable indicator of whether a stock is on track

---

17 Missed numbers are the earnings expectations that companies *fail* to achieve by analyst's consensus earning estimates.

18 Whisper numbers are those expectations of earnings that analysts do not formally project in written numbers but expect from companies whose guidance to analysts is usually on a conservative side of projections.

for earnings growth in the short run. Values indicating that a company is performing extremely well are a 1-Yr EPS Growth of equal to or greater than twenty-five percent (25 %) or greater. Companies achieving this level of growth have proven to the market that they have consistent positive upward earnings.

How did Ultrak's earnings perform in the current 12 months versus the prior 12 month period? Looking at Table 1, we can compare the EPS change in the current 12 month periods to the prior 12 months. This data was obtained from *www.wsrn.com*. We can observe that the Latest 12 mos. EPS change well exceeded the 25 % threshold level. It should be evident that most individuals prefer to simply locate this calculation on the web rather than calculate it as we have done. That is perfectly acceptable, and for purposes of illustration, I have chosen to show how this number was actually calculated to improve comprehension of the topic of short term earnings growth.

Table 1. Ultrak's Earnings Growth In current 12 mos. vs. prior 12 mos.

	FY'94 Q3	FY'94 Q4	FY'95 Q1	FY'95 Q2	FY'95 Q3	FY'95 Q4	FY'96 Q1	FY'96 Q2
EPS	$ 0.11	0.04	0.11	0.07	0.09	0.1	0.16	0.17
12 mos. EPS Total	‖‖➡			0.33	‖‖➡			0.52

$$\text{Latest 12 mos. EPS Change} = \frac{\text{EPS in current 12 mos.} - \text{EPS in prior 12 mos.}}{\text{EPS in prior 12 mos.}}$$

Solving using the data in Table 1,

$$\text{Latest 12 mos. EPS Change} = \frac{\$\,0.52 - \$\,0.33}{\$\,0.33} = 0.58 \text{ or } 58\%$$

In our Fundamental Model, those stocks whose 1-Yr EPS Growth is *greater than or equal to* 25% are assigned 25 points.

The information about Latest 12 mos. EPS Change or 1-Yr EPS Growth is readily available on a number of recommended financial web sites. However, the easiest way to find this value is using One Page Research and following the simple instructions in Figure 5.

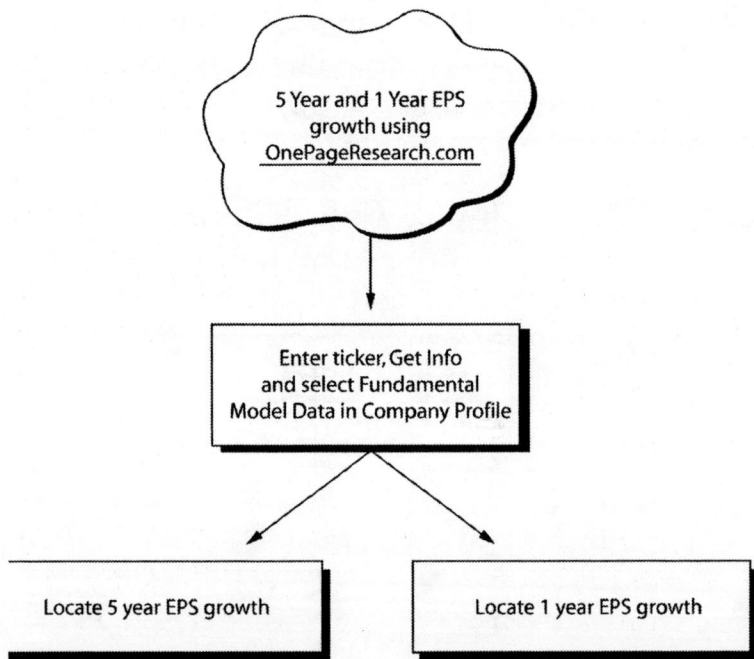

Figure 5. Locating 5 Year EPS/1 Year EPS

How Do Companies Succeed in Growing Earnings ?

Why is constant earnings growth crucial? *Those companies who deliver positive earnings growth over five years or over the latest twelve months are companies who possess the ability to generate increasing earnings per share over time.*

One or more of the following strategies are the most common methods for a company to grow stellar earnings over time:

✓   Reduce costs of goods sold
✓   Gain dominant market shares and hence increase volume
✓   Create innovative products in demand which allow pricing power for these new products
✓   Reduce long term debt
✓   Buy back outstanding shares and increases the earnings per share by fewer shares outstanding
✓   Acquire other companies with complementary strategies that are accretive[19] to the parent company

Ultrak utilized a combination of these strategies to effect short and long term earnings. Not only were they producing a large number of desirable products, they were also reducing costs and increasing profit margins. Recognizing that the demand for closed circuit TV's was growing globally, they acquired foreign companies to improve the manufacturing and distribution of their products while earnings from their company became accretive to their balance asset sheet as well.

Step 3: PS/R (Price to Sales Ratio or P/S)—Value Gauge

Let's switch gears from *growth* to *value* in using our fundamental model. Recall our model considers more than one value parameter, but

---

19 Accretive implies that an acquisition will produce *increased* earnings per share from the acquiring company.

it does weight some criteria more than others. Adding additional criteria to the model reduces risk inherent when only one selection criteria is employed.

As noted in Chapter 3, one of the most important single criterion for devising a winning strategy for finding stocks that outperform the broad market index of the S&P 500[20] is identifying stocks with a Price/Sales ratio less than or equal to 1.5. During an interview on CNBC with James P. O' Shaugnessey when he was asked about his stock selection research, he said "...*If an alien were to land tomorrow and ask you what is the most important thing to know about finding stocks within our universe that determines which stocks go up over time, you should answer in the appropriate language, Price to Sales Ratio.*"

The value of individual companies whose PS/R were less than or equal to 1.5 (PS/R = or < 1.5) should over time produce the best forward track record of performance according to back tested results from O'Shaughnessey.

Like O' Shaughnessey, I believe PS/R is the most important single value parameter. As a result, PS/R has a weighting of twenty-five percent (25 %) in our Fundamental Model. Recalling exactly what PS/R connotes, we can compute its value for Ultrak. The following figures were obtained from Barron's *Online* and were used to perform these calculations:

Price/Share in 12/95 = $ 5.00/Share[21]
# of Shares Outstanding in 12/95 = 7.37 MM or 7,327,000

---

20 S&P 500 is based upon a market-value weighted index of 500 blue-chip stocks, considered to be a benchmark of the overall stock market and composed from all sectors of the market.

21 In December 1995, $5.00 represents the *average* price/share. The stock ranged from a low of $4.50/share to a high of $5.50/share. Numbers for outstanding shares and Revenues or Sales were posted by the company as of December 29, 1995.

Annual Sales or Revenues in 12/95 = 28.7 MM or $ 28,700,000

Recalling our formula for determining PS/R:

Solving,

$$\text{P/SR(Price/Sales) Ratio} = \frac{(\$5.00)\ (7,327,000)}{\$28,700,000} = \frac{36,635,000}{28,700,000} = 1.28$$

In our Fundamental Model, those stocks whose PS/R are *less than or equal* to 1.5 are assigned 25 points.

Step 4: ROE (Return on Equity)—The Real Financial Picture for Investors

---

Return on Equity (ROE) is considered by many to be the best assessment of a stock or company's performance. Unlike earnings per share (EPS) which can be manipulated up or down by a number of accounting maneuvers, ROE is less affected by these tactics. If you recall from Chapter 3, earnings per share or EPS can be affected by three common factors. First, sale of assets for cash can occur, Second, a company reduces or suspends Research & Development spending, or Third, the ubiquitous statement of a *restructuring charge*[22] against earnings. All of these occurrences affect the closely-watched *bottom line*[23] or quarterly EPS tracked closely by analysts and institutional or large holders of the

---

22 Restructuring is a term in which the managers realize too many people are on the payrolls (layoffs lead to reduced fixed costs, and hence more net income) or the company intends an unplanned capital expenditure to maintain competitive.

23 Bottom line traditional refers to the profit after all expenses of the company are paid. Its location on the Income Statement physically appears at the end of the page.

stock. Shortfalls in projected earnings in the quarter are often a signal of a company's contemporaneous financial health, but can be misleading if the reasons for the shortfall or the quarterly EPS exceeding expectations are not clearly understood. Return on Equity (ROE) helps separate the signal from the noise.

$$\text{Return on Equity (ROE)} = \frac{\text{Yearly Net Income or Earnings}}{\text{Shareholder's Equity}}$$

Changes in ROE can be dynamic due to adjustments in quarterly profits. Therefore, it is often wise to use annual computations for ROE when evaluating a company's performance. After all, we are looking for companies with strong records of growth and increasing value. ROE is subject to change and is watched closely by value investors as a gauge of how well the managers of the company are performing their tasks in benefitting the shareholders. Stated another way, given the capital asset base charged to the managers of the company, how well are they performing as guardians of shareholder equity? Return on Equity (ROE) seems to measure this yardstick for managers' effectiveness reasonably well.

Let's look back at Ultrak's Return on Equity (ROE) in 1995 to evaluate managerial effectiveness.

Net Reported Net Income = $ 2,700,000
Total Stockholder Equity = $ 16,500,000

$$\text{Return on Equity (ROE)} = \frac{\$2,700,000}{\$\,16,500,000} = 0.164 = 16.4\%$$

In summary, many investors like Warren Buffett find ROE coupled with low or no long term debt to be a good indicator of how well the managers of the company are completing their stewardship of the shareholders' resources.

There are some factors affecting yearly net income or earnings, which in turn change ROE. Unusual aberrations of net income *upwards* can signal a sale of assets, a positive legal settlement, reduced spending on capital equipment, or reduced spending on research and development. Any of these activities can cause an extraordinary rise in net income per share which should be a warning for investors to perform due diligence[24]. Conversely, should net income show a significant *downwards* action, it can be attributed to sources such as lack of competitiveness, charges against earnings for restructuring, sale of assets at below original price paid, legal settlements, or excessive capital expenditures for plant modernization or a secondary offering of stock[25]. Whether or not a company revises its net income per share upward or downward, our model would reflect these changes.

In our Fundamental Model, stocks whose ROE is greater than or equal to 15 percent (15%) are assigned ten (10) points.

Step 5: Long Term Debt as a % of Equity—Financial Leverage for Stock Owners

A company's financial flexibility is often linked to its long term debt load and ability to repay that debt. A company's debt is rated by

---

24 Due diligence is the process where an investor looks closely at the information about a company before deciding whether or not to buy.

25 Secondary offering of stock or issuance of additional shares of stock is a common method for companies to raise capital for the company to retire debt, provide lower capital costs for expansion rather than issuing debt, etc. This often negatively impacts and reduces earnings per share since more shares are outstanding after additional shares are issued as a currency proxy.

Standard & Poors, Moody's and other investment sources reflecting the financial soundness of the company. Those companies with outstanding financial conservative postures are given the highest debt ratings and will command the lowest rates of interest on their debt issued as corporate bonds or other instruments of lending. Conversely, those companies with poor financial performance will have weak ratings and must pay higher rates of interest. Higher rates of corporate debt instruments are often referred to as *junk bonds*. High rates of return often signal that repayment of the principal may never occur. Companies that issue junk bonds put the corporation at risk since higher rates of interest must be paid first from net income.

Whenever a company has high levels of debt, it often limits the options of the company for expansion, acquisition of strategic resources, or expenditure of capital necessary to be competitive. Therefore, we look at the most common source of measuring a company's long term debt. Long term debt will include corporate mortgages that usually extend from one to eight years and excludes short term debt and liabilities. Debt/Equity Ratio or Long Term Debt as a % of Equity provides a better measure of a growing company's debt load. Most growth companies want to establish low values of Debt to Equity, but many have incurred significant corporate debt when they began fledgling operations. Growth companies with expanding earnings often reduce long term debt obligations to provide the necessary financial flexibility to use their cash for other projects, ideas or acquisitions which will in turn allow them to grow their businesses. The Debt/Equity Ratio provides investors with a tool to determine the ability of a company to deploy its resources more wisely. *Therefore, lower Debt/Equity Ratio values are desirable.* When comparing one company to another, end of fiscal year values are the most reliable indicators.

$$\text{Debt / Equity \% Ratio} = \frac{\text{Long Term Debt}}{\text{Shareholder's Equity}}$$

For Ultrak (ULTK), the values from *www.wsrn.com on 12/29/95* were:

Long Term Debt = $1,500,000
Total Stockholder Equity = $16,500,000

$$\text{Debt / Equity \% Ratio} = \frac{\$1,500,000}{\$16,500,000} = .0909 = 9\%$$

In our Fundamental Model, stocks whose LTD% Total Capitalization is *less* than or equal to 10 percent (10 %) are assigned ten (10) points.

Step 6: Institutional Ownership—Creating Awareness for Individual Stock Owners

Sponsorship of a stock consists of market makers[26], institutional investors, and money managers from mutual funds. The fact that institutional owners believe in the corporate story and the management's ability to execute specific strategies will lead them to buy huge amounts of stock. Companies often reveal their corporate strategies at analysts' meetings. These meetings are designed to educate potential owners and

---

26 Market makers are those brokerage companies who buy a large number of shares in a stock and resell them to individual investors. Carrying large blocks of stock in their inventory of overall holdings is often disclosed on stock transaction confirmations under the phrase, "We make a market in this stock."

encourage purchase of large blocks of their shares. Institutional investors are desirous to own companies with superior growth and earnings prospects. Purchase of stock in the early phases of growth and development of such companies affords the institutional investor a significant potential for stock price appreciation. Early adoption or purchase is critical for optimizing profitability. *Therefore, institutional ownership is necessary to drive a stock price up.*

Institutional ownership puts the stock on the investor's map and serves notice that support for the company and its strategy and potential for price appreciation is deemed very good. Many fund managers perform *institutional surfing*[27]. Each one wishes to know what the other is buying.

Author's Note:

An interesting consequence of institutional ownership below the threshold of 30% is that a percentage this low may be a good opportunity for the individual investor. Retrospectively, the discovery of Ultrak's stock was fortunate since it was below the radar screen of most professional investors. As time progressed, recommendations by market pundits for Ultrak occurred. This was followed by the purchase of large blocks of stock by additional institutional investors, which bolstered the price of Ultrak's stock over a relatively short period of time. *Keep in mind, if you are researching a stock with a low percentage of institutional*

---

27 Institutional surfing is the technique whereby money managers use *The Data Monitor*, a weekly published by William O'Neil & Co., which lists companies' stock performances, technical charts and shareholders.

*ownership, then perhaps the reasons it hasn't received institutional atten-
tion may not be immediately apparent to the individual investor.*

In our Fundamental Model, Ultrak's ISH (Institutional Ownership)
was 9%, *less* than or equal to 30 percent (30 %). Therefore, it was
assigned (0) points.

Economies of Scale, The Learning Curve and Great Management

(Optional Reading)

Corporate strategies are usually designed to *increase* sales or revenues, market share, and profits at the expense of their competitors. As
companies implement their strategic plans of operation, they travel
down the learning curve[28]. As a result, they should be able to produce
goods and services with ever *decreasing costs per unit*. This is also known
as *an economy of scale* whereby long production runs of manufactured
goods are produced at lower marginal costs. A simple example was
Henry Ford creating *economies of scale* by making cars in an assembly
line with a cost to end-use consumers of $850/car. Other cars made in
the same era were hand made and cost three to four times as much to
manufacture. With lower costs per unit, *increased* profitability should
occur. If the companies are producing superior products, coupled with
goods or services at ever lower costs per unit over time, then a dominant market share is established and even greater profitability follows.

---

28 Learning curve is referred to as the process of attaining lower costs of production for an individual item, good or service as time goes on. *This is often referred to as
coming down the experience curve.*

Case Study—Dell Computer (Summer 2001)

In the economic slowdown of 2000-2001, PC manufacturers faced a worse than anticipated decrease in shipments of what many had considered not only a mature, but a commodity business, i.e., personal computers. While overall global shipments of PC's decreased 2% from 2000 to 2001. During this time period, Dell's PC shipments *increased* 20% in the same time period thus pushing them into the #1 market share leader both domestically and globally. How were they able to accomplish this feat, and what were the consequences to their competitors?

First, increased demand for their PC's occurred because they lowered prices and competitors were unwilling to meet Dell's aggressive pricing strategy. The competitor's marginal cost[29] for comparable machines were significantly higher. Competitors selling at Dell's price would produce a loss on each unit sold.

Second, lower prices created new business taking market shares from competitors. Most importantly, they were doing so profitably.

Third, Dell's use of near JIT[30] (just-in-time) inventory systems allows falling component prices' for PC's to be passed onto the consumer in the form of lower prices. Dell has an inventory of only five days versus seven to eight weeks for competitors. Shorter inventory times mean lower supply costs to Dell. An interesting side effect of this

---

29 Marginal cost is the selling price where all fixed and variable costs are included. Selling above marginal cost is profitable.

30 JIT or just in time inventory means components are delivered almost as they are needed for final assembly of a manufactured item. This reduces inventory holding costs estimated to be 1% per month of an item kept in inventory and not used.

smaller inventory is that consumers reap the benefits of more cutting edge components.

Fourth, Dell's operating expense is half that of its rivals. This allows Dell to use its low-cost structure to gain market share by accepting lower *gross margins*[31] because demand at lower price points still produces greater profitability than its competitors. *Increasing* sales with lower gross margins can only can produce greater profitability if your marginal cost is the lowest in the competitive field. Dell's marginal costs were the lowest.

Step 7: Current Ratio (CR)—Safety Net for Companies and Investors

Finding companies with financial *solvency*[32] has always been a challenge for the individual investor. Many companies fail to pay attention to the needs of the balance sheet for short term situations, crises or unforeseen events that could potentially force the company to sell strategic assets in order to meet short term financial needs. Consider a current ratio (CR) as a measure of emergency readiness or source of funds in case opportunities or situations arise in the competitive environment. The current ratio takes into account a company's current assets and liabilities as seen in Table 2.

---

31 Gross margins are pre-tax net sales minus cost of goods sold divided by net sales, expressed as a percentage.

32 Solvency applies to a company ability to meet its short term obligations by its adequacy of liquid assets as they come due.

Table 2. Components of Current Ratio (Current Assets : Current Liabilities)

Current Assets	Current Liabilities
Cash	Accounts Payable
Cash Equivalents (Government and or Marketable Securities)	Short Term Bank Loans
Account Receivables	
Inventory	

$$\text{Current Ratio} = \frac{\text{Current Assets}}{\text{Current Liabilities}}$$

For years accountants have argued what the optimal current ratio should be. If the current ratio were 2:1, then a company only needs to liquidate one-half of its current assets to cover current liabilities. This has often been deemed as being fiscally conservative. A current ratio of 2:1 is sought after by investors as they search for companies with sound balance sheets. Interestingly, the average current ratio among most U.S. Corporations is 1.85:1, which is less than 2:1, but close enough to be considered acceptable.

For Ultrak, the values from *Barron's Online on 12/29/95* were:

Current Assets = $ 44,800,000
Current Liabilities = $ 34,900,000

$$\text{Current Ratio} = \frac{\$ 44,800,000}{\$ 34,900,000} = 1.2837 = 1.28$$

In our Fundamental Model, stocks whose current ratio is *less* than or equal to 2.0 are assigned ten (0) points.

Table 3. Fundamental Model Screen: Criteria, Informational Source, Ultrak Scoring.

Ultrak (ULTK) Fundamental Model Screen ...6/28/96

Parameter in Model	Criteria	Points Possible	Source of information	Actual Number	ULTK Points Attained
Earning Growth over past 5 years	>= 25%	25	*www.wsrn.com*	43 %	25
Earning/Share Growth in current 12 mos. vs. prior 12 mos.	>= 25 %	25	*www.wsrn.com*	58 %	25
Price / Sales Ratio or PS/R	=< 1.5	25	*Investor's Business Daily* Graph of ULTK on 6/28/96	1.28	25
Return on Equity	>= 15 %	10	*Investor's Business Daily* Graph of ULTK on 6/28/96	20.3 %	10
Long Term Debt as a % of Equity	<= 10 %	5	*Investor's Business Daily* Graph of ULTK on 6/28/96	9 %	5
Institutional Ownership	> 30 %	5	*www.wsrn.com*	9.2 %	0
Current Ratio	>= 2.0	5	*www.wsrn.com*	1.28	0
Total Points					90

Conclusion—Finding Confirmatory Analysis Stocks

As we complete our detailed scoring of Ultrak on 6/28/96, we recall this stock had an excellent chart pattern trending up. A fundamental score of 90 (See Table 3) and an excellent technical pattern made Ultrak a Confirmatory Analysis pick and winner! How has the company done since 1995? Well, I will let the reader look at a long term chart of the stock and decide. When to sell a stock for me has always been difficult, however, when the fundamentals deteriorate, it is time to sell. Unfortunately, the price chart of the stock often reflects that news sooner. Therefore, I 'm going to finish this chapter with Allan Harris's *four* rules of using technical analysis as a way for watchful investors to stay ahead of rapidly changing fundamentals:

Rule # 1. Buy Only Those Stocks That Are Going Up

The trend is your friend when it comes to technical analysis. Why would you want to buy stocks that have an upward pattern? If you are a risk adverse investor, then go with the trend.

Rule # 2. Look for Retracement of Up Trends

Look for those stocks that have exhibited a 25 to 50 percent retracement of previous up trends from their recent highs.

Rule # 3. Be On The Lookout for Obvious Breakout Buy Signals

Look for sudden upward price movements that produce a gap in the price pattern of the stock's chart.

Rule # 4. Know When to Leave The Party (Sell The Stock)

It is time to exit when the stock pattern exhibits a downward trend of lower lows and lower highs.

Chapter 6

Best Investing / Research Sites on the Internet

By James E. Farris, Ed.D.

> *We should be careful to get out of an experience only the wisdom that is in it, and stop there; least we be like the cat that sits down on a hot stove-lid. She will never sit down on a hot stove-lid again, and that is well; but also she will never sit down on a cold one any more.*
>
> *-Mark Twain*

Introduction

The purpose of this chapter is to give the reader a basic overview of Internet investing and to review some of the more useful and popular research web sites. After reading this chapter, the investor will have sufficient information which will enable him/her to: (1) locate and retrieve stock related financial information; (2) access web sites where critical information needed for technical, fundamental and *Confirmatory Analysis*[33] can be found; (3) obtain and/or update his/her investment education; (4) become acquainted with web sites that provide free historical and real time quotes; and (5) locate various investment financial calculators. In addition, this chapter will introduce the reader to the authors' web sites *www.confirmatoryanalysis.com* and *www.onepageresearch.com*. The appendix at the end of the chapter provides a directory of useful web sites and links for a more in-depth review of cyberspace investing. This chapter contains information for both the beginning novice and the experienced investor. Certain sections are written primarily for new investors and are designated *basic*. Experienced investors can skip these sections and proceed to the next sections.

The Internet is the latest modern day byproduct of the Information Age. What makes the Internet truly exciting is that it is interactive and it provides information on demand at the convenience of the user. The Internet is a vast world wide electronic library and repository of every conceivable kind of information which one can readily gain access through their home or office computer. Even though we are just in the infant stages of the Internet, it has changed the way we live and how we conduct business. Almost every publicly traded company now has a home page, most stock broker services have a web site and every stock

---

33 *Confirmatory Analysis* equally weights fundamental and technical interpretations for selecting outstanding growth and value stocks coupled with *technical analysis* to *identify* potentially winning stocks.

exchange has electronic links. So much investment information is now available that it would take a several books just to review the many web sites.

For the beginning investor, the Internet at first glance appears intimidating. However, with just a little use, its use will quickly become second nature. The Internet is currently the single best tool for gaining the latest information in the world of investing. Everything investors dreamed of having at their disposal just a few years ago is now on their computer. Before the age of personal computers, the main tools which independent thinking investors had at their disposal were a financial calculator, annual reports, research reports from brokerage houses, investment magazines, newspaper business sections, which were at best just a few hours old, and a few daily business news periodicals such as the *Wall Street Journal* or the *Investor's Business Daily*. Even Wall Street brokers had to rely on these same tools.

The very concept of purchasing stocks without going through a broker just a few years ago was unthinkable. The sole exception was through a company's dividend reinvestment program. Now there is an ever increasing trend to purchase securities through the Internet, thus bypassing the stock broker. This has lowered commissions and has saved the investor money. In addition, an increase in service and information has accompanied the use of discount brokers on line.

Not only can you buy and sell stocks through the Internet, you can monitor the price chart of a particular stock that you own or are considering purchasing as well as the stock's financial information. You can also read the latest financial news about world markets as well as news related to a specific company, such as announcements pertaining to stock splits or corporate quarterly earnings. In addition, you can review historical quotes and obtain real time quotes and read broker recommendations and earnings estimates. More important, you can continue your investment education and you can make money when you apply the knowledge you gain from the Internet. Although not technically an investment function of the Internet, communication with other investors is one of the most important reasons for using the Internet. The aforementioned are just a few of the numerous benefits which can be obtained from using the Internet.

The most frequently asked question is how to search the Internet for practical information. The first step is to purchase a reliable computer with sufficient memory and to select a reliable Internet access provider. Some thought and consideration should be made into the selection of an Internet provider. Monthly long distance costs, modem speed capability, reliability of the Internet provider and the ease of access and portability of telephone access are all-important items to consider. With the advent of cable modems and DSL, fast Internet connection speeds are preferred by investors. Less time is spent in waiting and more time is created for viewing financial sites. The ability of being able to access your Internet provider from other locations without additional charges is an important factor if you travel frequently. Once these issues are settled, then you are ready to get started.

Successful Internet investing, like traditional investing, involves discipline and the use of sound investment methodology. Successful investors are motivated to keep up-to-date in the investment world. The only significant differences between using the Internet to search for investment ideas and former methods, such as reading broker reports that arrive in the mail and a broker, are the speed and the means whereby one obtains research, company information, the exchanges of ideas and placing buy and sell orders.

You have spent enough money purchasing computers, printers, and obtaining an Internet service provider and investment books. The author's goal is to help you maximize your investment resources by using the free information on the Internet. Generally the information is paid for by the sponsors of the web site and banner advertisements. The major advantage of doing on-line research is that the amount of time to screen stocks is reduced dramatically. What once took hours, now can be completed in minutes. In addition, by using the Internet, current information levels the playing field for all investors.

The web sites discussed in this book are mostly free. Some contain both free and fee-based services, for example, *Wall Street Research Network, www.wsrn.com*. One of the goals of this chapter is to present several web sites where the user can obtain the necessary fundamental and technical variables for free. Two or more web sites will be mentioned wherever possible in the event that a site becomes a fee-based site in the future or the wed site goes out of existence. All the web sites referenced have been in existence for three or more years. As a reminder, be sure to bookmark important Internet web sites. This will make it easier to locate and retrieve financial information related to publicly held companies.

Search Engines (Basic)

If you are a novice at using the Internet, it would be a good idea if you would take the time to familiarize yourself with some of the Internet search engines. Search engines are software programs that search the Internet for data. Three of the most popular search engines are: *Excite, www.excite.com, Lycos, www.lycos.com* and *Yahoo!, www.yahoo.com*. *Yahoo!* is probably the most widely used search tool for researching financial information pertaining to individual securities.

Keep in mind a few simple rules when using a search engine. First read the instructions on using the search engine under consideration. Use just a few key words when you are researching information on a particular stock. Generally it is a best to place quotation marks around the key words. This will assist the search engine in narrowing the scope of the search and it will shorten the time it takes to receive data. For example, if you want to obtain data on sheet music, do not enter the words sheet music without using quotation marks. The search engine might insert the conjunction *and* between the words. As a result, you stand a high probability of receiving extraneous information on such things as bed sheets, pop music, country music, etc. Instead, enter "sheet music." The same rule applies if you are attempting to find information on a stock. If you were attempting to locate information on *Sun Microsystems* (SUNW), enter "Sun Microsystems" with quotation marks in order to avoid obtaining information on the sun in the sky and computers in general.

Investment Education Sites (Basic)

Three good sites to obtain free investment education are *Morningstar, www.morningstar.com, Investor's Business Daily, www.investors.com* and *Equity Analytics, Ltd., www.e-analytics.com.* All sites are easy to use and all will provide you with sufficient information to help you obtain a solid investment education.

Morningstar is probably the most comprehensive educational web site. This is a must read section for the novice investor. However, the experienced investor can further his education as well. You can truly never know enough concerning investments. Just enter the URL and when the home page appears, click on *University*. Go to the *Investment Classroom* and explore the site. You will be delightfully surprised at the information provided for free. In addition, *Morningstar* provides useful fundamental analysis information on individual securities. You are encouraged to examine the many features of this site.

In order to take advantage of the *Investor's Business Daily* (IBD) website, you must register. After registration is complete, you can explore the site. When the home page appears, click on "IBD Learning Center." There you can review numerous subjects on security investments. To view any module, just click on the module's title. If you are a beginning investor, you should definitely review the glossary of investing related terms and words.

To use *Equity Analytics, Ltd.*, click on the subject *All About Stocks* and you will find sufficient information to assist you in gaining a basic understanding of stock market terminology, technical analysis, investment principles, etc. In addition, you can review reports on technical analysis software as well as download software at no charge. You can also read and review ten educational glossaries on investing. This site contains a host of useful investment information for both the novice and experienced investor.

General Reference Sites

Both the novice and experienced investor can take immediate advantage of *InvestorLinks, www.investorlinks.com.* This is a good site to gain experience in surfing the net, especially if one is not familiar with navigating the Internet. This site is recommended because of its numerous links to other financial and stock related web sites. If you like to read the financial sections of newspapers, or if you want to subscribe to any of the numerous on-line financial newsletters, newspapers or magazines, you can easily do so by clicking on the newspaper(s) of your preference. If you want to obtain information related to mutual funds, option or future investments, just click on the appropriate link.

Locating Recommended Stocks

Before one begins the screening process, a list of stocks to be screened has to be obtained. There are several places where one can initiate the prospecting process depending on the personal interests of the investor. For example, if an individual has a preference to research the technology sector, he might turn to a brokerage house which follows the technology sector. He could also review some of the electronic or print newsletters which covers the technology sector for their recommendations or he might review some of the on-line magazines for their technology picks. On the other hand, if the investor has no particular sector preference, he could start with one of the many brokerage firms recommended stock lists or the lists mentioned in a particular investment newsletter or web site.

The following is a partial list of the URL's that provide a list of recommended or historically performing stocks. There are numerous web sites which one could inspect. The ones mentioned in this chapter will provide you with a representative sample on what is available on the Internet. Remember that you can always obtain a list of recommended stocks from any brokerage house. Several of these firms have their recommended stocks listed on their web site, for example, *Merrill Lynch, www.ml.com.*

Another site that you might want to review is *Active Investment Research, www.stockresearch.com.* This site offers a free Internet investment newsletter, *Timely Investment Mailing List,* which provides a list of recommended stocks along with links to a more complete summary of the companies under consideration. One other site worth mentioning is *Market Guide Investment Center, www.marketguide.com.* The home page for this site has a link to its *What's Hot/What's Not* page which contains a list of the hottest sectors, hottest industries and hottest stocks in selected price ranges.

News Stories and Historical Stock Prices

Most investors want to know the latest news on stocks they own and/or are considering buying. There are numerous sites to check for daily news stories. *Yahoo!, http://finance.yahoo.com/* and *Wall Street City, www.wallstreetcity.com,* are two of the more popular sites. Enter your stock symbol and click on *news.* Clicking on the headlines will give you the complete story. Probably the best site to obtain a historical quote is *Wall Street City.* Enter the URL and click on *Stocks* and then enter the ticker symbol and select quotes.

Real Time Quotes

For those individuals who have a need for real time quotes, there is a handful of free sites that one can use. *MoneyCentral, www.moneycentral.com* and *Wall Street City, www.wallstreetcity.com,* will meet this need. Both sites require you to register to take advantage of this feature.

Fundamental Analysis: "What to Buy?"

The use of fundamental analysis gives an investor the means of filtering a large group of stocks in order to obtain a small list of stocks that have the potential to outperform the market in general. The importance of fundamental analysis and the major key financial ratios, which one needs to carefully evaluate a company, were presented in previous chapters. The following web sites contain the most important financial variables for conducting fundamental analysis on a particular stock by utilizing free information from Internet web sites.

Wall Street Research, www.wsrn.com, has the best free comprehensive fundamental data that can be obtained from the Internet. *Wall Street Research Net's* site gives the investor five years of fundamental financial ratio data to review. Five years is sufficient time for the investor to determine if a long term trend is underway, ending or possibly just beginning. *Wall Street Research Net* has six of the seven parameters needed to use the *Confirmatory Analysis, www.confirmatoryanalysis.com, Fundamental Model Calculator. Yahoo!'s, http://finance.yahoo.com/,* web site contains five of the seven variables.

Table 1 indicates the fundamental variables that can be found on the aforementioned web sites needed to use the free *Fundamental Model Calculator* in the *ConfirmatoryAnalysis.com* web site.

Table 1. Internet Location of Fundamental Model Parameters

Site	5 Year EPS Growth Rate	Latest 12 Months EPS Change	Price/Sales Ratio	Return on Equity	Long Term Debt as a % of Equity	Institutional Ownership	Current Ratio
www.wsrn.com	✔	✔	✔	✔	✔	✔	
http://quote.yahoo.com			✔	✔	✔	✔	✔

Technical Analysis: "When to Buy, How long to Hold... When to Sell?"

Technical analysis deals with graphic representation of a stock's performance over time and its pattern interpretation for determining the future direction of the stock's price. Chapter 2 provides a good overview of technical analysis. This section will describe free web sites where good technical data and charts can be easily located and understood. As a word of caution, a sudden drop or rise in the price of a stock, as reflected on a stock's chart, may be due to some financial anomaly such as a stock split. The authors suggest that investors review both fundamental and technical analysis data on any security they are considering purchasing or selling.

RedHerring, www.redherring.com, is a good site for the novice investor to gain an understanding of technical analysis charts. The experienced investor will also find *RedHerring* a quick site to obtain baseline information of how a stock is performing. *RedHerring* provides an easy to understand one year chart which compares a stock to the popular S&P 500 index benchmark. To use this site, click on the URL and enter the ticker symbol for the stock and click on *Go*. After you have reviewed the chart, return to the option frames to select from *Detailed Quote, News, Profile & Financials, SEC Filings, Earnings History.*

Big Charts, www.bigcharts.com, is one of the most comprehensive free technical chart sites on the Internet. It is a highly sophisticated site that provides the experienced investor with numerous charting options. The novice investor will discover that this site will provide an opportunity to experiment with various technical parameters as he becomes familiar with technical analysis. *Big Charts* gives the viewer three chart options, *Quick Chart, Interactive Charting*, and *Java Chart*. Novice investors may find it helpful to use *Quick Chart* until they obtain a greater knowledge of technical analysis.

Enter a stock symbol and click on one of the chart options. *Quick Chart* gives you a twelve-month easy to read charts. Above the chart is information pertaining to the trading of the stock under investigation. In addition, there are links to the company's annual report, SEC filings, brokerage reports, etc. *Interactive Charting* and *Java Chart* gives experienced investors numerous options such as *a time frame, compared to, indicators* and *chart styles*. The *time frame* category gives the option to have a chart ranging from one day to one decade. You can also choose the frequency of the chart. The *compared to* feature compares a stock with several indices such as the DJIA or you can compare the stock with several other stocks. The "indicators" allow you to select moving averages, Bollinger Bands[34], price channels, volume and several other indicators. The *chart style* gives you the option of bar charts, candlestick charts and the chart background along with several other options. *Java Chart* has the same features as *Interactive Charting* with the addition of examining daily buying volume.

ConfirmatoryAnalysis.com

Confirmatory Analysis is a special fundamental and technical screening process whose origin was derived from an examination of two complementary investment disciplines. *Confirmatory Analysis* uses fundamental and technical analysis to identify stocks with the greatest potential for price appreciation. Fundamental analysis looks at a company from the perspective of growth and value. Technical analysis examines a chart pattern to determine the direction of a stock's price movement. *Confirmatory Analysis* uses a template model of importantly weighted fundamental factors to achieve a numerical score in order to

---

34 Bollinger Bands - A technical analysis chart trend described by John Bollinger using moving averages. Bollinger Bands are plotted as plus or minus 2 standard deviations over a 200 day moving average based on closing prices.

determine if a company is a "buy" on a fundamental basis. Combining a high score > or = to 75 coupled with an upward trending technical chart pattern gives the investor a stock worthy of further research.

The *ConfirmatoryAnalysis.com* web site has been designed to be complementary for readers of *Confirmatory Analysis: Finding Winning Stocks*. You are encouraged to investigate this web site as it will assist you in advancing your investment education and experience by accessing the Internet to research stocks. Directions on how to use the *Fundamental Model* and *PFT ELS Calculators* are provided on the web site.

Key Features:

✓ Free Financial Calculator for Fundamental Model screening
✓ Provides fundamental numerical scoring based on investors' research of fundamental parameters as outlined in Chapters four and five
✓ PFT ELS *Analyzer*
✓ Hot links to *Big Charts*, *Wall Street Research Net*, *Quicken*, *Zacks Research* can be found on *One Page Research*
✓ A suggested reading list of books and other helpful web sites for stock research
✓ Subscriber area for quarterly/semi-annually authors' confirmatory analysis picks
✓ An interactive e-mail link to authors for questions and comments

The site is easy to navigate and very user-friendly. Enter *www.confirmatoryanalysis.com*. When the home page appears, read the menu and click on the selection of your choice and follow the directions. There is also a *Contact Us* area which will allow you to write the authors, ask questions or to make comments. If you plan to use the *Fundamental*

Calculator, input your variables from the *Basic Confirmatory Analysis Work Sheet.*

Company Reports: Tying It All Together

You can obtain the annual reports on many companies using the Internet. The easiest method is to enter the URL for the company you are researching. Many companies are now going to an on-line annual report. Unfortunately not every company has a web site and not every company that has a web site has their annual report on their site. If the company does not have a web page, you might order a free annual report by using *The Public Register's Annual Report Service, www.prars.com,* site. Another alternative is to enter the URL for *Barron's Annual Report and Earning Service, www.worldinvestorlink.com.* This is a free service. *Barron's Annual Report and Earning Service* also provide a toll-free number 1-800-965-2929 where you can order annual reports. If you can't obtain an annual report from the company's web site or if you can't order it from *Barron's* or *The Public Register's Annual Report Service,* you can still contact one of the numerous on-line brokers and request them to send you an annual report.

Although not technically an annual report, you can still obtain much of the same company information, minus the photographs and charts, by reviewing the company's 10-K's filings with the *Securities and Exchange Commission (SEC), www.sec.gov. All companies are required to report their financial information to the SEC. The SEC in return has placed every publicly traded company's 10-K information on its web site. To review a company's 10-K, enter http://www.sec.gov/cgi-bin/srch-edgar. When the SEC's EDGAR page appears, type in the name of the company you are researching and click enter. As a word of caution, every document that the company has filed with the SEC will appear. Scroll down until you find the company's latest 10-K report and click on the same.*

Things to look for in a company's annual report or its SEC 10-K include the company's corporate strategy, corporate profitability, return on share holders' equity, competitive advantage over competitors, global market position and global exposure in terms of sources of revenue and profits.

International Sites

Corporate Information, *www.corporateinformation.com*, is considered to be one of the best sites to examine companies for both privately held and publicly traded foreign and domestic companies. The site is organized by country names and most countries have linked sites. It is one of the best sites to obtain fundamental financial information, a company's competitors by profitability. *Corporate Information* is a very comprehensive web site and is one of the easiest sites to navigate.

If you are seeking foreign stocks listed on the NYSE as ADRs (American Depository Receipts)[35] , *www.adr.com* is your best choice for research of market sectors, charts and company specific information, news, etc.. Screening of foreign equities and creating an International portfolio make this a must bookmark site. For investors wishing to lower their overall risk through diversification overseas, this is your site for finding stocks.

Internet Calculators to Help You Answer Stock Trading Questions

There are several questions that all investors should attempt to answer prior to purchasing and/or selling a stock. For example,

---

[35] ADRs are negotiable certificates issued by a U.S. bank representing a specific number of shares of a foreign stock traded on a New York Stock Exchange. Companies must confirm to U.S. Financial Accounting Standards Bureau to be listed as an ADR.

questions such as: what is the percentage of commission I will pay, how much profit will I make or loss will I incur if I sell now, what is the expected dividend return rate, how will exchange rates' affect foreign stocks I own, how long will it take to obtain a return on my investment, how will profits affect my taxes, how volatile is the stock I am considering buying, etc. Many investors will not attempt to answer financial questions because they either don't have a financial calculator or don't know or understand the mathematical formulas. The solution, use on-line Internet financial calculators to help obtain the answers to investment questions. Two of the best sites where stock and financial calculators can be found are *MoneySearch*.com, *www.MoneySearch.com*, and *Robert's Online Applications, www.intrepid.com/~robertl*. To use, enter the URL and click on "Calculators." *Robert's Online Applications* is a good site for comparing commission costs for on-line brokers based on the number of shares bought and sold. *Robert's Online Applications* has been cited in the Investors' Corner section in *Investors' Business Daily*.

Brief Overview of Key Web Sites

Big Charts, www.bigcharts.com, is the best overall free technical chart site on the Internet. This site has already been discussed in the chapter. If you are going to perform technical analysis, then this site should be one of your bookmarks.

Microsoft's MoneyCentral, www.moneycentral.com, was recently ranked the number one financial web site by Barron's. It ties with the financial news television station, CNBC, and its one-stop shop financial services make *MoneyCentral* a leader. You can track your own stocks, do online research and read columns by written by leading financial analysts. *MoneyCentral* has a computer stock ticker that you can download to your personal computer. *MoneyCentral's* features are too numerous to mention.

Morningstar, www.morningstar.com, has both free and fee-based services. It is one of the best sites to obtain an on line education on investing. If you invest in mutual funds, then this site is for you. *Morningstar's Quicktake Reports* is an excellent source for fundamental financial variables and easy to understand color charts.

Quicken, www.quicken.com, is a multifaceted web site that covers just about every area of financial services. *The Investments* and *Stocks* web pages provide a listing of a company's competitors, current EPS, estimated quarterly earning and other useful date such as comments pertaining to various aspects of the company's business. Also you will find information pertaining to the company's financial condition, taxes, sales channels, acquisitions, etc. In addition, if you want to review the stock's chart, *Quicken allows you to compare the company under consideration with other companies plus the S&P 500, NYSE and NASDAQ. You can also plot moving averages and you can select a chart for designated time periods ranging from a week to five years.*

TheStreet.com, www.thestreet.com, is noted for its founder Jim Cramer and other outstanding financial columnists. The site has both free and fee-based services. It has links to numerous financial tools, calendars of financial important events and columns on variety of investment subjects.

Wall Street Research Net, www.wsrn.com, has both free and paid subscription pages. However, the free pages contain an abundance of fundamental information which both the novice and experienced investor will find useful. One of the major strengths of *Wall Street Research Net* is its link to numerous investment web sites. For the avid researcher who likes to do perform due diligence with fundamental research on publicly traded companies, this is a good web site to use.

Yahoo!, http:// finance.yahoo.com/, is one of the best overall financial web sites. It allows the investor to have one or more stock portfolios to track stocks. It is easy to navigate and has unique features such as a tax center. The site allows you to quickly obtain company news, read the profile of the company under consideration and to check fundamental ratios. It has links to the company's web site, interesting financial links and event dates pertaining to the company's earnings.

Conclusion

As you can easily see, the Internet is the best stock investment research tool the individual investor has ever been given. Even with this fantastic tool, it takes discipline to do due diligence research and to use the web sites in a methodical manner. You can make money if you apply what you learn and you can lose money if you don't develop a systematic approach to investing. If you can follow the approach mentioned in the book and use the web sited mentioned in this chapter, you will be able to effectively screen for stocks that have the potential to be outperforming investments.

Appendix: Additional Internet URL's for Reference and Research

Domestic Stock Exchanges

American	*www.amex.com*
Chicago	*www.chicagostockex.com*
NASDAQ	*www.nasdaq.com*
New York	*www.nyse.com*
Pacific	*www.pacificex.com*
Philadelphia	*www.phlx.com*

European Stock Exchanges

Geneva	*www.bourse.ch*
London	*www.stockex.co.uk/aim*
Paris	*www.bourse-de-paris.fr/*
Germany	*www.exchange.de*

U.S. Government

Security & Exchange Commission	*www.sec.gov*
Federal Reserve Board of Governors	*www.federalreserve.gov*

Investment Related Magazines

Business Week Online	*www.businessweek.com*
Barron's	**www.barrons.com**
Business 2.0	*www.business20.com*
Fast Company Magazine	*www.fastcompany.com*
Forbes	**www.forbes.com**
Fortune	**www.fortune.com**
Investor Guide Weekly	**www.investorguide.com**
Inc. Magazine	**www.inc.com**
The Industry Standard	*www.industrystandard.com*
Kiplinger Online	*www.kiplinger.com*
Money Magazine	*www.money.com*
Red Herring	*www.redherring.com*
Smart Money Interactive	*www.smartmoney.com*
Stocks & Commodities	*www.traders.com*
MIT Technology Review	*www.technologyreview.com*
Upside Magazine	*www.upside.com*
Worth Online	*www.worth.com*

Chapter 7

PFT ELS® and Technology Stock Investing

By Richard J. Davis, M.D., M.B.A.

Setting a goal is not the main thing. It is deciding how you will go about
achieving it and staying with that plan.

-Tom Landry, football coach

Introduction

This chapter presents a unique concept that examines technology stocks on factors other then their price, earnings, P/E, volatility or capitalization size. The concept is called PFT ELS, or Profit Elasticity which represents a measure of corporate efficiency and productivity. PFT ELS may serve as a proxy for productivity. PFT ELS is a measure of the relationship between 5-Yr Earnings Growth and 5-Yr Revenue or Sales Growth. Its origins in microeconomics will be traced *(brief optional readings are present for those interested in a crash course in microeconomics, but can be omitted)* as well as its B-School [Business School] theory origins. PFT ELS can assist an investor in determining whether or not technology companies are: (1) emerging; (2) near the Tipping Point[36] of success and advancing; or, (3) are falling backwards as competitive pressures occur. Calculation of PFT ELS will not require a financial calculator but only a PC with an Internet connection.

There are seven identifiable forces which shape PFT ELS. *Technology companies have embraced these powerful forces to generate a global competitive advantage.* We will examine the origins of PFT ELS, its definition, application and FAQ's (*F*requently *A*sked *Q*uestions) in order to gain an understanding of the use and applicability of PFT ELS in investment decisions.

Identifiable Forces that determine corporate productivity and PFT ELS

1.   Use of scale economies to reduce cost per unit produced

2.   Ability to amortize research and development costs over large production runs

---

36 Malcolm Gladwell, *The Tipping Point*. New York, New York: Little & Brown, 2000. Concept refers to the principle of exponential growth, the idea that the new amount of some quantity being measured is proportional to the initial amount rather than constant [linear] increases. This is captured in the mathematics that describes how epidemics spread, populations grow [well known to Malthus more than a century ago], radioactivity decays, and so on. This idea can be demonstrated in an epidemic when the ratio of infected/non-infected exceeds one the infection will spread rapidly; hence, it has passed the *tipping point*.

3. Reduction of variable costs from either outsourcing or reduced supplier and or component costs

4. Reduction of unit labor costs through use of technology itself

5. Reduction in operational or fixed costs per unit of goods/services produced or manufactured

6. Global currency devaluations producing a positive impact on reduction of costs for production of finished goods inventory

7. Low inflation/interest rates promoting corporate capital expenditures and increased deployment of less expensive technology to enhance corporate efficiency

How these forces interact and enhance corporate productivity will be explained in detail later in this chapter.

Origins

PFT ELS has its origins in microeconomic theory. For those students who were bored with Econ 101, demand theory, production and cost analysis, and pricing policies based on marginal costs, you will be relieved to hear that we will not annoy you any further. For the readers of this book who yearn to find the relevance and applicability of microeconomic theory to stock investing, and specifically to fundamental analysis, your rewards are close at hand. Business school academics always proclaim the importance of classical economic theory to real world investing as "*...How should I know what all this means to investing in real companies?*"

Proponents of modern economic academic theories find themselves challenged when their theories are applied to the U.S. Economy (Macroeconomics), and, more specifically, their interpretation towards the Theory of the Firm[37]. It is not the inconsistencies of the academic microeconomic theories that fade, but rather, it is the lack of quantitative mathematical models which are necessary to understand and perhaps to some degree explain the subtleties of defining productivity in the U.S. Economy. Corporate productivity clearly improves earnings, but defining it has been an elusive as Monty Python[38] or Indiana Jones[39] attempting to find the Holy Grail. Nonetheless, productivity is the foundation whereby companies have grown revenues or sales and hence, earnings dramatically. Other subtle effects of corporate productivity produce reduced wage pressure demands, and when coupled with lower inflation for goods and services result in U.S. companies becoming more globally competitive. To confirm the elusive nature of measuring corporate productivity, Alan Greenspan, our Chief Economist, has publicly stated that he cannot figure out what is going on behind the numbers, nor explain what improved productivity means. I will make no attempt to second-guess Dr. Greenspan, however, I will attempt to propose a fundamental analysis theory that provides an indirect measurement of corporate productivity. These are easy to measure and allow a comparison of two or more companies .

Definition

> PFT ELS *is a quantitative measurement of a company or stock's overall productivity in achieving incremental profitability based on compounded revenues or sales growth over five years or the normal duration of a corporate business cycle.*

---

37 *Theory of the Firm* is often found in the explanation for the course description of microeconomics.

38 *Monty Python* refers to a famous group of comedic British Actors in the early 1970s.

39 *Indiana Jones,* portrayed by Harrison Ford, is the hero in several adventure movies.

I will attempt to define classic investment measurements examining the use of PFT ELS as a tool for understanding technology stocks. For the time being, read the definition again and tuck it away in the back of your head.

Investor Traditional Understanding and Measurement

If we take a traditional investor's approach to understanding PFT ELS, then we will see its basis and simplicity as a proxy for assessing corporate productivity. There are at least three reasons why you should consider its use for assessing technology companies. *First*, PFT ELS has tremendous relevance to technology investing because it *recognizes the five-year time horizon of traditional business cycles. Second*, PFT ELS applies classic microeconomic modeling theory to the technology sector. Technology stocks represent an important economic force within the U.S. Economy. These companies constantly change, adapt to the marketplace, and evolve more quickly than companies in other sectors of the economy. *Third*, it is important to set some parameters in assessing and monitoring companies which do not often conform to traditional fundamental analysis investment criteria. Failure in comprehending the prominent companies within this sector has often been cited as a reason for not investing money into companies whose goods and services cannot be easily explained to others. Many missed opportunities in emerging companies have seen investors simply shrugging their shoulders quietly saying,"...*I wish I had bought Cisco (CSCO), Microsoft (MSFT), Intel (INTC), Sun Microsystems (SUNW) and others before their prices skyrocketed upwards,...and sold them before they fell.* "

Traditional Five Year Business Cycle vs. Technology Business Cycle

Admittedly, the five year classical business cycles may not be applicable to all technology stocks. The traditional business cycle implies a boom to bust usually over five years. The reason is that it takes approximately five years to allow product introduction, development, market share gains, leading to product maturity. Afterwards, market share declines as competitors enter the marketplace and ultimately drive prices downward as product obsolescence occurs. Traditionally, these events occur over five years. However, when we refer to technology stocks, five years may have seen many product business cycles wax and wane. The complete cycle of events for products produced in technology might be better reflected in shorter cycle times. The life span of technological innovations and products are usually measured in months rather than years. Therefore, *the technology business cycle is shorter than the traditional five year cycle.* Such a cycle has often led investors to place technology stocks under the mistaken category of cyclical stocks similar to the steel or auto industry sectors.

Traditional undervaluation using P/E (price to earnings) relates to historical boom or bust cycles present in the U.S. Industry as a whole. Using P/E ratios therefore becomes a futile way to either value or follow technology companies. Similarly, using PEG ratios (Current P/E ratio / projected EPS growth for the current fiscal year) has been often recommended for finding companies who may possess good business prospects for the future. Difficulty can arise using such measurements. For example, when to sell a stock if its ratio gets higher or to buy more stock if the ratio gets smaller? No clear guidelines exist. Only an expectation for increased earnings growth in the future will create a demand for investors to purchase the stock at ever higher valuations of its traditional P/E or PEG ratio. This explains why *earnings momentum* drives stock prices higher than normally accepted market valuations, based on a stock's P/E or PEG ratios.

Uncertainty always clouds the future expectations of technology companies. Andrew S. Grove, CEO of Intel, in his seminal work, *Only the Paranoid Survive*, defined this concept well. "*You need to plan the way a fire department plans: They cannot anticipate where the next fire will be, so it has to shape an energetic and efficient team that is capable of responding to the unanticipated."* This is due in part to the extremely competitive nature of the business with rapid development and deployment of products where businesses either fail or go onto new heights. (See Figure 1.)

Technology Stock Survival Curve...

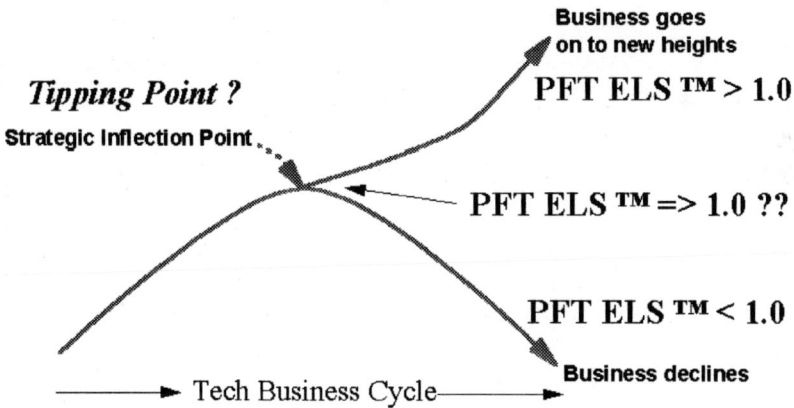

Business goes on to new heights
PFT ELS ™ > 1.0

Tipping Point ?

Strategic Inflection Point

PFT ELS ™ => 1.0 ??

PFT ELS ™ < 1.0

Business declines

Tech Business Cycle

Concept Source: *Only the Paranoid Survive,* A.Grove, CEO, Intel

Figure 1.

Business School Theory into Practice...

American Industry has shifted from a manufacturing economy in the late 1950s to one where innovation has occurred with the invention of the microprocessor in the late 1970's and deployment of the PC in the early 1980's. This is currently being followed by the development of the information age with its revolutionary new technology which links those *wired* via networking and the Internet. What are the drivers for these technology-based companies? What maneuvers are they utilizing, based on Business School theories, throughout the United states and overseas?

Admittedly, many Wall Street pundits have difficulty understanding these stocks because they clearly do not understand their core competencies and hence, the potential for their future profitability. Recent volatility in technology stocks, as seen in the Summer of 1996 and Fall and Winter of 1997, have made many Wall Street sages find these stocks to be a difficult investment to evaluate. *What are the learned lessons from B-Schools that technology stocks use on a daily basis?*

Shortening the product cycle from years to months was the first lesson technology company applied to the marketplace. Improved and newer products for the dollar spent on technology goods are all outgrowths of classical business school theory. *One does not need to understand demand curves to realize that lowering the price point for consumers or companies to purchase technology increases demand for these products.* Henry Ford understood this fact when he produced the Model T. In today's business model, let's use the innovation of the sub $1,000 PC as an example with the goal of a sub-$500 PC on the horizon. In their first year, these low-priced computers garnered 40% of all new computers sold! As the Model T created the new automotive industry, the sub $1,000 PC is now creating a whole new category of buyers and lending credibility to the information technology industry. As the competitive bar with lower PC prices is raised, this leads to reduced profit margins among fewer companies that are capable of producing lower-priced computers at a profit. Consolidation with fewer players also occurs as competitors exit specific product segments due to failure of profitability. Toshiba's exit from the home desktop computer market is a good example of this process in action. Most likely, if the long touted Network PC's truly develop into a usable computer below $500, another explosion will ensue as the demand will truly outstrip supply.

Second in turn, new channels of distribution have made direct selling from business to business and from business to consumer commonplace. This has continually lowered the ultimate price to the purchaser of those goods and services. Passing cost savings to the customer has been a popular incentive for using this method. Whether a major Fortune 500 corporate customer purchasing 1000 computers, routers, network products or just one individual buying one computer, the direct model pioneered by Dell and Cisco has been emulated by many in the technology industry such as Gateway, Compaq, and IBM.

Third, Dell's use of *Just In Time* (JIT) component delivery and flexible manufacturing to customize computers that are already sold reduces inventory. In turn, this reduces inventory holding costs and increases inventory turns (more units produced and sold).

Fourth, improved logistical systems for delivery (overnight/next day delivery) have placed the product on the customer's desktop immediately. Personal productivity, utilization and the benefits derived from this technology deployment are simply additives to the benefit of these products.

Fifth, Internet commerce has created an easier ordering mechanism that does away with the need for human intervention. Such a system reduces labor content and costs of placing orders. Transaction costs per unit are significantly *decreased*. When one looks at 1996-7 Internet Commerce figures by the Top 10 companies on the web, the diversity of products and services approach $ 5.78 billion in annual revenue or $ 483 million/month. (See Table 1.)

Table 1. 1996 Sales on the Internet
Internet Commerce[40]—Transaction-Based Web Sites
Annual/Monthly Revenue

Company	Business Line(s)	Online Annual Revenue	Revenue / Mo
Cisco	Network products	$ 2,880 MM	$ 240 MM
Cendant	Consumer products	$ 1,088 MM	$ 61 MM
Dell Computer	Personal computers	$ 730 MM	$ 60 MM
America Online	Computer services	$ 464 MM	$ 38 MM
Gateway Computer	Personal computers	$ 150 MM	$ 12.5 MM
E*Trade	Securities trading	$ 148 MM	$ 12.3 MM
Amazon.com	Books on line	$ 112 MM	$ 9.3 MM
Peapod	Groceries	$ 60 MM	$ 5 MM
1-800-FLOWERS	Flowers , gifts	$ 48 MM	$ 4 MM
Auto-by-Tel	Auto shopping	$ 14 MM	$ 1.2 MM
E Bay	Auctions	$ 5.74 MM	$ 475 K
Top 10 Total		**$ 5,794 MM**	**$ 483 MM**

A Mini-Course in Microeconomics....Keeping It Simple

(Optional Reading)

The concept of demand curves regarding customer behavior was alluded to when I stated that demand for lower priced and highly valued technological goods/services, such as computers, often leads to *increased demand* as the *price is lowered*. This is also known as the

40 Mary Meeker. " *Internet Quarterly: The Business of the Web*," Morgan Stanley Press, 1997.

Classic Law of Demand. Interestingly, this holds true for many other goods and services beyond those produced by technology stocks. If we recall some algebra, we recognize $Q = A + BP$ as a linear equation where Q is quantity demanded, A is the influences of all other independent variables, B is the coefficient of P, Price. Solving for P, then yields $P = A + BQ$ (Figure 2 .) Note that the numerical value of B is expected to have a negative sign. This is due to the inverse relationship of *increased* goods demanded as price *decreases*. Note: The line is sloped *downward* due to the negative sign of B. This is due to the Law of Demand (Figure 2). As we travel along the demand curve from Point A to Point B, we note that prices move *downward* from P1 to P2, and the initial Quantity demanded at Q1 *increases* to a greater Quantity demanded at Q2 (Figure 2). This is the basic reason that items placed on sale decrease existing inventory. In times of low inflation, a wealth effect is created, prices remain constant, and the demand curve is shifted to the right. (See Figure 3.) Quantity of goods is *increased* from Q1 to Q2.

Classic Law of Demand Theory

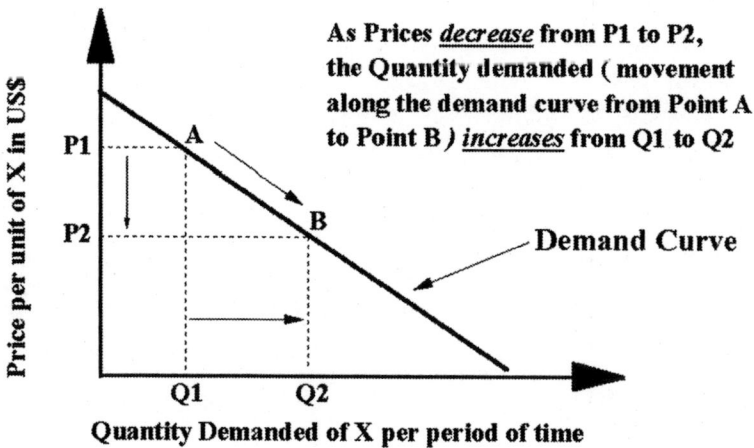

Figure 2.

Law of Demand Theory with low Inflation and Constant Prices

As Prices remain constant, low inflation produces a so-called *wealth effect* which stimulates a shift in the demand curve to the right and and *increased* quantity demanded from from Q1 to Q2

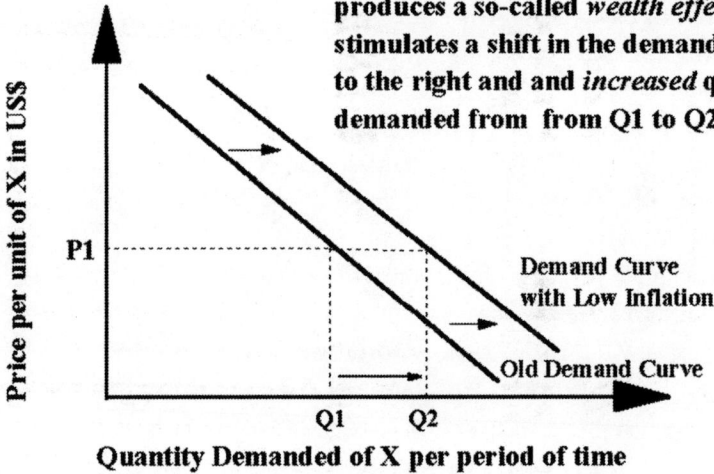

Demand Curve with Low Inflation

Old Demand Curve

Quantity Demanded of X per period of time

Figure 3.

How Technology Companies Lower Costs, Gain Efficiency...Improve Productivity

As technology companies put Business School theories into practice, they gain a number of key competitive global advantages over an ever *decreasing* product life cycle of specialized goods. As a result of implementing these theories, the *seven identifiable forces* previously discussed forge the framework of corporate productivity. PFT ELS is an indirect measure of this productivity as well as a quantitative tool that reflects the aggregate effect of these forces.

HINT: *As you read each force, attempt to recognize the cause and effect relationship between costs, revenues and ultimate corporate profitability.*

First, economy of scale is the ability to *reduce* prices per unit produced over time with increased production. Non-technology companies have accomplished this feat well. Autos, appliances and other electronic goods such as televisions are excellent examples of the mass production benefits to the consumer. With PC prices falling, can two computers in the home be far behind? Three computers? Economies of scale produce reduced costs per unit. In a competitive marketplace, consumer *prices decrease* actually *increases* overall demand for goods and services. It is the inherent efficiency of production which has *increased* output of technology companies with lower costs. With technologically innovative products, companies create dominant market shares. In turn, this leads to *increased profitability through increased sales or revenues.* The first Ford Model T cost $850. A few years later, the price had dropped to $250. Who were the real beneficiaries, Ford, consumers or both? From 1987 to 1997 prices for personal computers dropped (due to improving technology) from $2,000 to less than $1,000. (See accompanying graph Computer Prices vs. Purchases in Figure 4.)

Computer Prices Vs. Purchases

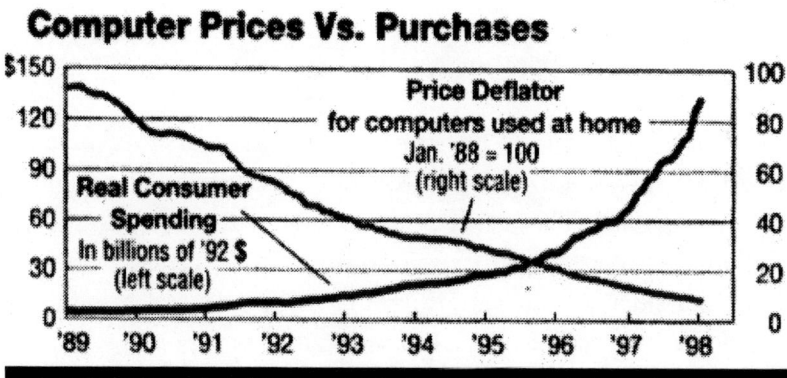

Figure 4.

Second, amortizing large research and development costs over larger production runs has significantly reduced the overall price of technological innovative goods such as Internet routers, networking hubs, as well as semiconductor and telecommunication chip development. Fewer development costs per unit of goods and services sold enables a company to recoup these expenses faster. Lower R&D costs per unit produced provides *improvement of operating income or net operating margins* by driving ever increasing demand for technology goods and services. Both the producer and the end-use consumers of these technological goods will benefit. *Remember how the cost of handheld calculators dropped over time?*

Third, companies are able to achieve reduction in their variable costs from either outsourcing or reduced supplier and/or component costs. Outsourcing is when specialized companies design or manufacture component parts for OEM's (original equipment manufacturers). Component parts are incorporated into larger products that bear the name of a recognizable company. Both companies benefit from this exclusivity of selling/buying of high quantity and quality components that are subsequently incorporated into complex technological goods. Again, the ultimate beneficiary is the consumer of these goods through lower costs. With the Cost of Goods Sold (CGS) lessened, *more profit per unit of goods/services is available via gross operating margins. Have the TV, VCR, and other electronic items become cheaper or more expensive over time?*

Fourth, productivity from utilizing technology reduces unit labor costs of goods or services produced. Admittedly, a very difficult number to get one's arms around. This can be expressed in the reduced amount of human labor content per unit of good or service produced. Nowhere in the annual report or company financials will you find this figure. We hear about a company's laying off workers' in corporate mergers and downsizing, but rarely learn of the number of new skilled workers hired. It is difficult indeed to assess the leverage created from existing and new hired workers through the use of enabling technology. Getting more out of less from those in the work force appears commonplace. One can see it in the office setting through voice and/or e-mail. Engineers in technology companies using Parametric Technology's (PMTC) Pro/ENGI-NEER® CAD/CAM (computer assisted design/computer assisted manufacturing) systems use technology to improve product cycle development time and actual manufacturing time of finished goods. Therefore, *less* unit labor cost/unit of goods or services produces *increases* in the moneymaking capability of these companies. *What do you think is the impact of Internet commerce aided by technology? Its future for business to business commerce and business to consumer commerce?*

Fifth, technology can lower fixed costs per unit of goods/services produced or manufactured. How is this feat accomplished? One of the largest fixed costs of a company are comprised of those administrative costs which include costs for *S*ales, *G*eneral, *A*dministrative (SGA), identified as items on the balance sheet. Technology companies are among the first to embrace techniques that reduce costs per unit of goods/services sold. As companies become lean and mean operational units, Internet sales dominate those from more traditional selling methods (e.g., phone, fax, and personal orders). In most technology companies, these *fixed costs*/unit of goods and services sold are *decreasing* which can contribute substantially to *net income* or the bottom line of a company's balance sheet. *How does Internet commerce benefit the consumer?* Hint: *Internet transactions reduce cost. Discount online brokers' commission charges for securities trading online is a fraction of a full service broker enacted transactions.*

Sixth, global currency devaluation can have a positive impact despite lost sales due to higher prices of goods produced to overseas buyers. On the surface, higher prices imply reduced sales due to decreased demand. However, this creates a situation where efficiency and reduced cost of goods produced can potentially lead to higher profits. This may not make sense at first, but let me explain further.

During the Fall of 1997, an unusual sequence of events began unraveling in the Far East regarding currency devaluations of Thailand's *baht*. Similar concerns regarding other Asian economies spending more money than tax revenues and other export income generated. Investor concerns about the currency valuations in Singapore, Malaysia, Hong Kong, Korea and even in staid Japan increased. When the smoke had cleared, it was observed the value of invested capital in these countries had significantly declined. Investor confidence had been shaken and the U.S. Dollar emerged as the global currency. The U.S. Dollar had *appreciated* most in the wake of foreign currency devaluation. This effect produced crisis and panic around the world in all financial markets. Although this was a problem overseas, an impressive correction in the U.S. Market ensued. The Dow Jones 30 Stock Index was down ~7% plunging 550 points in a single day! *If the problem were overseas, what was causing the problem in the U.S. Markets?* The culprit was the uncertainty of future earnings generated by U.S. Companies in goods and services already sold and projected in the future to Asian countries. Our exports would be more expensive, due to depreciation of most Asian currencies relative to the U.S. Dollar. Many multinational companies' (e.g., Proctor & Gamble, Coca-Cola) stock prices were impacted significantly downward. Technology stocks were the leading sectors of the 1997 Stock Market to this date. However, tech stocks were now the most negatively impacted in terms of price due to expected loss of revenues or sales. Almost instantly among the doomsayers of technology stocks, a contrarian view began emerging.

✔ Key Point:

Careful analysis revealed that many technology companies would actually become beneficiaries of the negative Asian currency devaluations.

How could this be so? A downturn in a stock's price often accompanies bad news, and the news was dismal. However, amidst the chaos, those companies with large Asian component suppliers were reevaluating their position. On the surface, this seemed like bad news, but suddenly turned into a bonanza for many technology companies. A number of subtle factors were behind the optimism. Current and future sales of finished goods would surely be in question. However, closer examination revealed that most Asian countries comprised only *single digit percentage sales* of U.S. Technology Companies. Asian currency devaluation meant that price of U.S. Technology Goods in the Far East would be *increased* or more expensive. This in turn would *reduce* demand. Remember Demand Curve Function in Figure 3? Here was clearly a case for applied economics. Yes, some business would be lost due to a stronger U.S. Dollar and weaker currency in these Asian Countries, but how would sales in the rest of the world be affected?

As financial analysts began worrying about the loss in sales and profitability of U.S. technology companies business in the Far East, a positive note began arising as the corporate and green eye shade types analyzed the real impact of the situation. *Michael Dell, CEO of Dell Computers announced during an interview on* CNBC *that 6% of Dell Computer's sales were in the Far East, but 70 % of their component costs were also there.* Of course this meant that some lost sales due to higher prices goods would occur. However, the costs of assembling those finished goods with components such as computer memory chips, motherboards, modems, disk drives, and monitors would be *significantly cheaper* since those outsourced goods to foreign manufacturing sites in the Far East would *decrease* the overall cost of computers manufactured and further widen gross operating profit margins due to lower Cost of Goods Sold (CGS). *Can you predict the impact of this unusual circumstance on other U.S. technology companies? How do you think this affects their global competitiveness on a cost basis in the global markets? How will the end-use consumer be affected by the reduced cost of technology goods?*

Seven, low inflation rates promote corporate capital expenditures and increased purchase of high technology finished goods. A similar occurrence happens when the individual has to spend less of his/her income on paying interest on debt. This promotes the so-called *wealth effect*. Borrowing costs are lower and hence more income is freed up for other purposes. This is true for both corporations as well as individuals. To gain a competitive edge, adoption and deployment of technology becomes a mandate. Most companies strive to gain a market share for their own respective goods and services. Therefore, careful and selected use of increased technology deployed produces incrementally lower costs of production and higher marginal revenue and profit. *Let us look at the individual to better understand this concept. First, the effect on consumers' behavior is very similar to corporate mentality given a low inflation environment. Second, as interest rates fall, demand for homes increases. The refinancing of existing homes frees up monthly income from mortgage interest payments. Does the average consumer save the money saved from higher interest payments or spend it? On what? Similarly, corporations act like individuals. They also desire to move up a competitive notch by using excess cash flow for major capital expenditures of technology that will in the future afford them a better competitive position with a lower cost structure of production. What will be the impact on corporate as well as personal consumers of technology goods consumed?*

Demand Theory in a Low Inflation Environment

(Optional Reading)

Even if the price of technology goods is held constant, another shift in the demand function occurs with *ceteris paribus* or all other things considered the same. Low inflation produces *greater* disposable income due to *decreased* interest paid. The demand curve is then further shifted to the right, with an *increased* quantity of demanded goods/services despite prices remaining constant. This fact holds true for those individuals and companies alike who are seeking to become more productive and competitive. (See Figure 5.)

Law of Demand Theory with low Inflation and Constant Prices

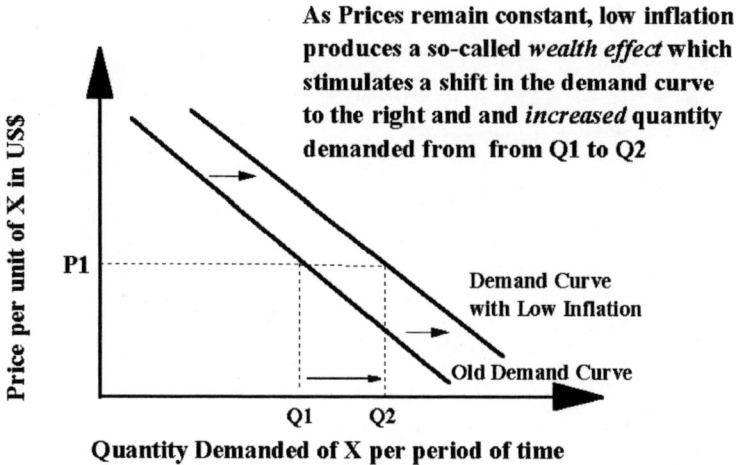

As Prices remain constant, low inflation produces a so-called *wealth effect* which stimulates a shift in the demand curve to the right and and *increased* quantity demanded from from Q1 to Q2

Price per unit of X in US$

P1

Demand Curve
with Low Inflation

Old Demand Curve

Q1   Q2

Quantity Demanded of X per period of time

Figure 5.

Author's Note:

Although not shown in Figure 5, can you predict the effect of deflation on the quantity of technology goods or services demanded? Try to sketch this effect with a pencil on Figure 5 as lower prices occur. HINT: *What happens on the Old Demand Curve with low inflation? Answer: It is shifted to the right.* In essence, the inability to affect price increases (known as deflation) has the indirect effect of subsequently *lowering* prices while *increasing* the demand for goods and services further. Thus, low inflation is leveraged as a driver for *increasing* amounts of technology goods produced and demanded.

In summary, the *seven forces* discussed have been very important for the success of U.S. technology companies. Therefore, what is really happening as evidenced in the forces and factors above is a unique blend of a dual pronged strategy: *(1) constantly lowering costs through efficiency and hence productivity for ever larger quantities demanded and produced while (2) increasing earnings through decreased costs inherent to the finished goods and services of these technology companies.* It is this degree of productivity that we are seeking to measure and compare technology companies with each other to determine their long-term viability, and increasing profitability over time.

Explaining this complicated phenomena will be achieved in the next section on *elasticity.* The concept of PFT ELS will afford the reader insights into evaluating and comparing technology companies in a way not previously considered. One can use this measurement to help make decisions when constructing a technology portfolio and during the due diligence process *before* buying any company. Conversely, once the decision has been made for stock purchase, PFT ELS can provide a useful parameter for following these companies without the uneasiness of price volatility. Let's go back to basics.

What Does Elasticity Really Mean ?

Elasticity is a principle widely used in economics and expresses the responsiveness of one variable to another variable. To be exact, *elasticity is the percentage change in the dependent variable occasioned by a one-percent change in an independent variable.* Classical economics has many derivations on the elasticity theme such as price, income, point, arc and income elasticity to name a few.

PFT ELS Explained

PFT ELS is a more globally defined term that incorporates the seven identifiable forces into a single measurement of corporate productivity. PFT ELS shows the proportionate response of Earnings Per Share to a *one percent change* in sales or revenues. The time period for this observation is five years. This represents a broad but easily measurable parameter that defines those companies whose success in improving productivity and efficiency ultimately affects their earnings growth and price appreciation over time.

Calculating PFT ELS, Earnings Per Share is the *dependent* variable and sales or revenues is the *independent* variable.

$$\text{PFT ELS} = \frac{\% \text{ change in } dependent \ variable \text{ (EPS growth or earnings per share)}}{\text{One \% change in } independent \ variable \text{ (Revenues or Sales growth)}}$$

PFT ELS utilizes the past five years Earnings or compounded Earnings Per Share Growth expressed in percentages divided by the corresponding Sales Growth or Revenues over the same period. The result of this division yields an expression which determines the *overall incremental percentage rise in earnings per share (EPS) for each one percentage point of Sales or Revenue growth over the comparable five-year period.* Mathematically, this can expressed as follows:

$$\text{PFT ELS} = \frac{\text{5 Yr EPS \% Growth Rate}}{\text{5 Yr \ \ Revenue or Sales \% Growth Rate}}$$

Note: Negative values of either revenue growth or earnings per share *nullify* the use of PFT ELS.

Author's Note:

Within a specific industry sector or SIC (Standard Industry Code) those companies with the highest PFT ELS values exhibit superior productivity. Relative to their peers, they tend to be the strongest company in a given sector of pure play companies. It is recommended that readers use PFT ELS as one of your financial ratios in performing due diligence in your equity research. It is imperative that it should not be used alone, but in concert with other similar measurements of financial solvency and growth.

In calculating PFT ELS, there are many financial sites on the web listed in Chapter 6 which include the numerical values necessary to compute the simple calculation. However, following the flow diagram in Figure 6 using One Page Research will save time in this process.

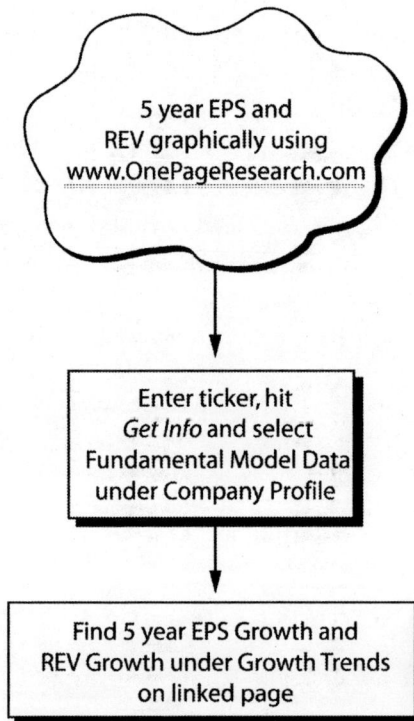

```
  ╭─────────────────────────────╮
  │   5 year EPS and            │
  │   REV graphically using     │
  │   www.OnePageResearch.com   │
  ╰─────────────────────────────╯
                │
                ▼
  ┌─────────────────────────────┐
  │   Enter ticker, hit         │
  │   Get Info and select       │
  │   Fundamental Model Data    │
  │   under Company Profile     │
  └─────────────────────────────┘
                │
                ▼
  ┌─────────────────────────────┐
  │   Find 5 year EPS Growth and│
  │   REV Growth under Growth Trends│
  │   on linked page            │
  └─────────────────────────────┘
```

Figure 6. Finding 5 Year EPS and 5 Year REV Growth

Finding and Running the Numbers...Sample Calculation of PFT ELS using SUNW

Let's run a sample calculation of PFT ELS with data obtained from recorded from 04/06/98.

5-Yr EPS Growth Rate   = 42.46 %
5-Yr Revenue Growth Rate = 17.8 %

$$\text{PFT ELS} = \frac{\text{5 Yr EPS Growth Rate \%}}{\text{5 Yr Revenue Growth Rate \%}} = \frac{42.46\ \%}{17.8\ \%} = 2.39$$

Before we analyze Sun Microsystem's PFT ELS = 2.39 we need to take a look at some of the concepts that will make this number meaningful, and easier to understand. Let's look graphically at the historic EPS and REV Growth over the past 5 Years for Sun Microsystems over the period in question. (See Figure 7 and 8.)

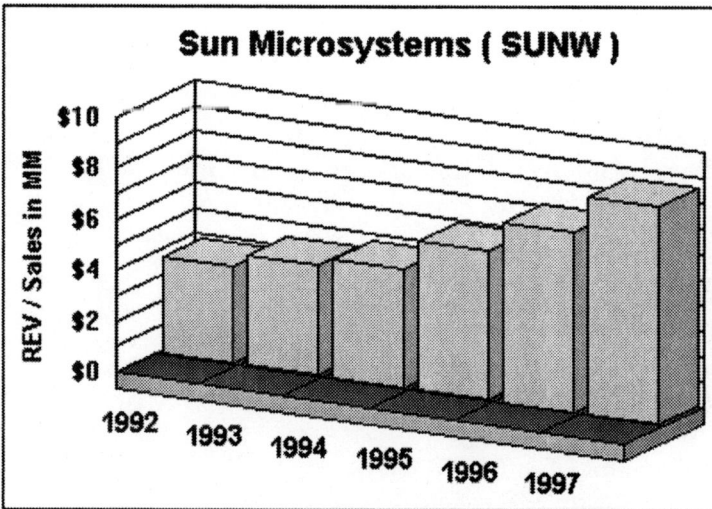

Figure 7. Five Year REV from 1992-1997

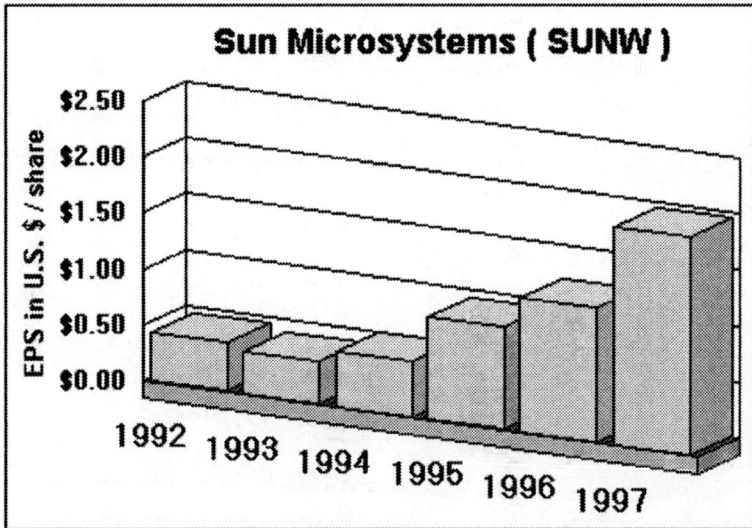

Figure 8. Five Year EPS from 1992-1997

Graphical Interpretation of Sun Microsystems EPS and Revenue Growth 1992-7

If the reader simply looks at Figure 7 and Figure 8 depicting 5 Yrs Revenue and EPS respectively during the years 1992-1997, we see that both are going up over time. That is obvious. Briefly reflect upon these simple questions: *Can we discern divergence in their respective up trends since both seem to be increasing over time? By visualizing the charts, can we determine the mathematical expression about the pattern of their growth?*

Understanding PFT ELS—A Simple Exercise

(Optional Reading and Exercise)

This exercise is designed to demonstrate underlying principles and relationships between EPS and REV growth over five years. Take a soft lead pencil and place a large dot on top of each bar in both figures 7 and 8. Now connect the dots. *What is the pattern of their respective growth patterns?* (No, an aardvark will not appear, relax. This is not one of those tests.)

Connecting the dots in Figure 7 demonstrates an almost straight upward line because revenues or sales are *increasing* incrementally over time. This is known as a *linear* function. On the other hand, connecting the dots in Figure 8 shows a *curved* upward line of *increasing* earnings over time. Do you recognize this pattern? Mathematically, equations for such lines are called *exponential* functions. If we translate the function or relationship of the two lines, we might verbalize the following:

Are Accelerating Earnings Growth Attractive to Investors ?

Recall the Earnings Momentum discussion in Chapter 5? Does Sun Microsystem's 5 Yr EPS Growth % represent a positive component in the Fundamental Model under the category of Earnings Growth? If you answered *yes* to both questions, you are becoming a very discerning investor. Learning to recognize the subtleties and being able to interpret the growth patterns of EPS and Revenue will improve your chances of finding winning stocks. Gaining pattern recognition in your mind imprints the key variables that successful companies must possess in order to attract investors. Once drawn to the stock through ownership, good news spreads fast among institutional and individual investors. This should produce price appreciation over time, especially if the relationship remains intact between revenue growth and increasing earnings.

I highly recommend visualizing graphs of a company's EPS/REV over a five-year period to assist you in grasping the concept behind PFT ELS. *Follow the easy to use steps on Figure 9 to locate this information for companies you are investigating on .*

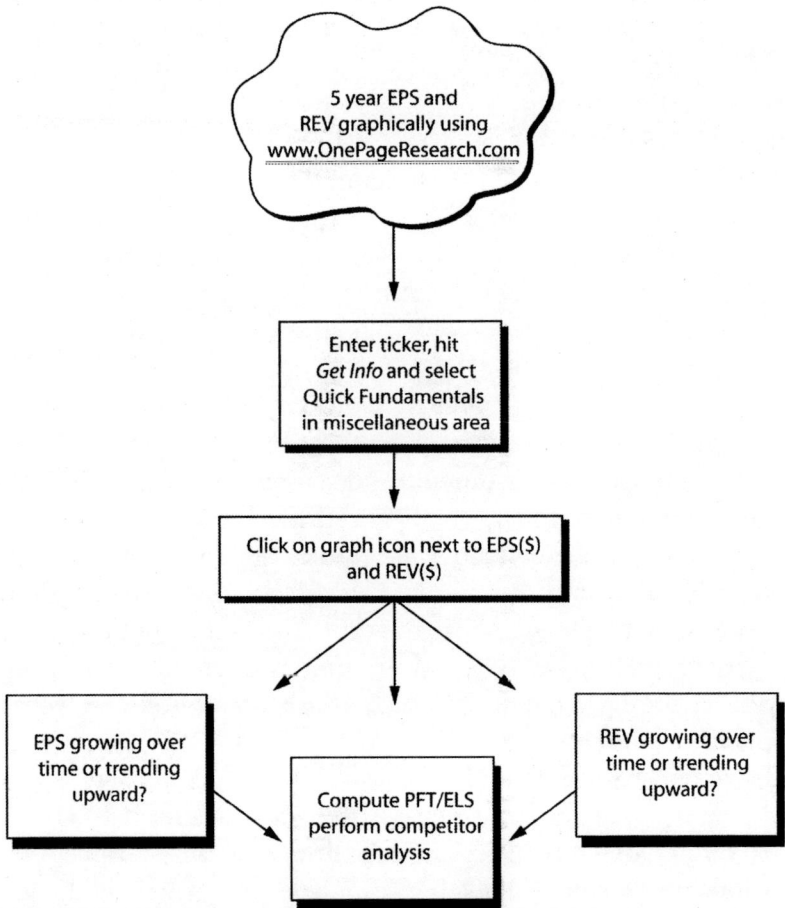

Figure 9. Graphics of 5 Year EPS and 5 Year REV Growth

Interpreting the Rise and Fall of PFT ELS

After computing PFT ELS for a company, the next step is comprehending exactly what it means. In our example of Sun Microsystems,

PFT ELS in 1998 was equal to 2.39. Over the *five-year period (1992-1997), each one percent in revenue or sales growth generated incremental earnings growth of 2.39 percent.* If Sun Microsystems were to increase its PFT ELS, then earnings per share would increase as function of revenue growth times PFT ELS. Consider PFT ELS measuring the efficiency or productivity of a specific company's ability to grow earnings.

Rising Values of PFT ELS

Companies with *rising* values of PFT ELS have to become productive by *increasing* profitability while *reducing* costs of producing their goods or services. Employing one or more of the seven identifiable forces will improve a company's productivity which in turn will produce an *increasing* value of PFT ELS. Those companies who have moved their earnings from a linear to an exponential growth have reached their *Tipping point* and are at the apex of their success. When PFT ELS is rising over time, investors can withstand the price volatility inherent with the technology sector. This is where investors need to be patient and await the market to recognize and value these companies accordingly.

Falling Values of PFT ELS

Should the value of PFT ELS for a company fall, then the investor will possess an early warning sign that something has changed. When PFT ELS *decreases* it may signal one or more of the following events: (1) Competitors are entering the same playing field and are more efficient; (2) Competitors are gaining market shares by improving their profitability and their PFT ELS; or, (3) Change in corporate strategy has occurred, such as an acquisition that loses money. As a result of falling PFT ELS, the company may be losing some of its hard earned productivity gains that provided a differential advantage in the marketplace and stellar earnings in the past.

In summary, following PFT ELS values over time should produce a direct measure of productivity for a technology company. Whether the values are *decreasing, increasing* or remaining constant, the investor should monitor a company's PFT ELS to determine a trend.

Quick Test: Determine Sun Microsystems' PFT ELS at the time of reading this chapter. Has it increased, decreased, or remained the same? How has the price of the stock changed?

PFT ELS *Critical Values…Equal to or Greater Than 1.0*

If a technology company is successful in leveraging itself by growing greater earnings percentages incrementally with smaller sales or revenue growth percentages, then its PFT ELS values often equal to or exceed 1.0. In the previous chapter, you read about the *Tipping Theory* and its relevance to those companies whose PFT ELS values exceed 1.0 and why these companies gain market dominance. Those technology companies who attain PFT ELS of greater to or equal to 1.0 have arrived in a unique position of preeminence. Conversely, when calculating PFT ELS values, those companies with values less than one can mean one of two events.

1.   The company is still climbing up the curve of PFT ELS .

2.   A company with declining or eroding value of PFT ELS potentially signals a technology company whose sustainable product differentiation has been lost to its competitive peers. We can summarize these concepts in Table 2.

Table 2. Interpretation of PFT ELS Values

PFT ELS® Values	Significance
PFT ELS < 1.0	Emerging Company or a competitive loser to its peers
PFT ELS = 1.0	A company at the Tipping Point
PFT ELS > 1.0	Market dominance achieved, sustainable competitive advantage accomplished

Technology Stock Survival Curve with PFT ELS ®

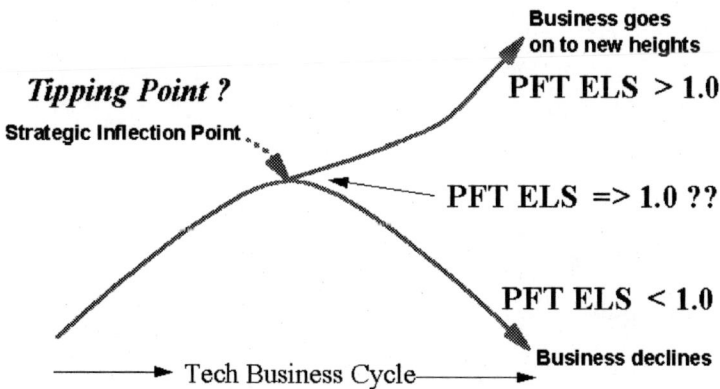

Concept Source: Only the Paranoid Survive, A.Grove, CEO, Intel modified
by Dick Davis using PFT ELS ® financial ratio analysis

Figure 10.

If we recall Figure 1 near the beginning of the chapter presenting the Technology Stock Survival Curve, we might modify Andrew Grove's Strategic Inflection point where PFT ELS = 1.0 and visualize the Technology Business Cycle in Figure 10.

Using the PFT ELS *Analyzer on the Web Site*

Another simple way to determine the significance of PFT ELS values is to determine a company's 5 Yr EPS Growth and 5 Yr Revenue Growth on the web sites mentioned in this chapter and then travel to and Click on PFT ELS Analyzer.

PFT ELS FAQ's (*Frequently Asked Questions*)
(*Optional Reading*)

Question: What is the best way to utilize PFT ELS *once I have determined it ?*

Answer: What is PFT ELS telling you about the company? If it was less than 1.0 (PFT ELS < 1.0), then is this a company that is climbing up the curve of prosperity. On the other hand, is it a company sliding back down the curve? Reviewing price charts of the company in conjunction with its PFT ELS will usually answer this question. Of course, in times of recession, or severe Bear Markets (= or > 25 % retracement from highs), use of PFT ELS in evaluating companies may have minimal value other than to confirm those tech stalwarts or find emerging companies whose competitive advantage over time is sustainable and leads to rapid EPS growth.

Question: Why use five years in calculating PFT ELS ?

Answer: Five years is the traditional economic business cycles of boom and bust. If one looks at companies surviving over five years rather than a single year the likelihood in assessing a company's survivability is significantly better. Five years of transacting business in competitive markets sorts out the weaker players. Success or failure to sustain new products, innovations, attain market shares, and hence profitability, generally occurs in this time frame. Companies like Microsoft (MSFT) and Intel (INTC) had a successful beginning, but only after they had proved their viability in this critical time window. It was not until that time did non-speculative investors purchase their stock.

Using a five-year horizon to measure PFT ELS provides an assessment of companies and their success in incrementally increasing earning with sales or revenues. This process of efficiency and productivity does not occur overnight. It takes time to achieve these gains, and time to sustain the process once success has begun. It is doubtful that unless shock waves were to occur in either prices or other factors (competition quitting or exiting a business) that measuring earnings and sales over a few quarters or even a single year would provide any value to really assess the long term viability of these technology companies. In addition, the Tech Business Cycle is not the usual one product produced by a company spanning over a year or two, but instead, it is an array of sophisticated technological goods and services constantly being customized to the end user with every decreasing product/service life cycles measured in months.

Question: Can I use PFT ELS *if the value of 5 Yr EPS or Revenue or Sales Growth were negative at the beginning of the five-year observation period? Can I use the* PFT ELS *valuation as a predictor of a company making a turn around if the company had a negative value at any point during its 5 Yr Earnings Growth?*

Answer: No, strictly adhere to the definition of PFT ELS *"...Negative values of either revenue growth or earnings per share in year one (starting place of revenue/eps determination) or year five (ending place of revenue/eps determination) nullify the value or use of PFT ELS."*

NOTE: Due to the mathematical computations necessary to determine PFT ELS values, change from negative to positive earning per share produces erroneous 5 Yr EPS Growth determinations.

Only by following the company over time can one determine whether or not the year in which earnings were negative had a significant impact on the company for the long term horizon. You might miss an opportunity to invest in a turn around stock, but there are plenty of stocks with better prospects.

Question: Why use PFT ELS for evaluating technology stocks?

Answer: This is a great question. Investors searching technology companies may be more concerned with earnings growth than traditional value parameters for selection. Technology stocks can possess *both* outstanding *growth* and *value.* Valuation of technology companies, according to traditional stereotypes using P/E, often creates companies with relatively high values of P/E relative to the overall market. As a result, investors can sit on the sidelines and watch these stocks catapult upwards in price one day and suddenly without warning fall into the abyss. Price volatility is often magnified in technology companies. Uncertainty clouds investor decisions on whether to hold or sell their technology stocks. If individual investors are unable to constantly evaluate the impact of news, earnings and competitors' prowess, a mutual fund specializing technology is reasonable. However, if individuals wish to hold individual stocks rather than a large number of stocks, PFT ELS can provide one of many valuable tools to separate the signal from the noise. PFT ELS provides an easy to measure value which can assist investors in monitoring the progress or failure that may signal the time to sell or purchase more of an individual stock or watch it patiently as the price seems to ride the roller coaster up and down.

Question: Can stocks with PFT ELS < = 1.0 *undergo significant price appreciation?*

Answer: Yes, with some qualification. This would represent a situation where a company's PFT ELS was < 1.0 despite apparent price appreciation. One should ask the following question: *What is the company's strategy for use of profits or net income?* In some cases, it is capital spending on the infrastructure for the future. In other cases, it may be that the company is buying or acquiring other companies and proprietary intellectual property using the currency of its stock. Such efforts will often produce a relatively flat PFT ELS over time despite the market welcoming such acquisitions and rewarding the company stock price for its forward thinking in remaining at the cutting edge of technology. Another variation on this theme is the fact that although revenues or sales may be growing due to acquisitions, it may take time for these acquired companies to be accretive[41] to earnings. (Remember: Revenue growth is the denominator and earnings growth is the numerator of PFT ELS.)

Question: In general, is it advisable to simply watch stocks with PFT ELS *values less than 1.0 rather than purchase them because stocks whose values of* PFT ELS *are* < 1.0 *can signal a loss of competitive position?*

---

41 Accretive to earnings refers to *increased* earnings over time due to the acquisition of a company. The length of time necessary to produce increased earnings can be variable.

Answer: If we are comparing two or more companies with similar business lines or products, and our competitive analysis showed them equal, then buying the company whose PFT ELS = or > 1.0 might produce the tie-breaking vote of confidence to purchase. Those companies who have reached the *Tipping Point* and have established unique competitive advantage with increasing profitability relative to their peers, often are the leaders in their industry or sector.

Conclusion

Hopefully, the reader has added yet another tool to his/her financial ratio tool box for evaluating technology stocks! The purpose of this chapter has served to link the importance of earnings growth relative to revenue or sales growth. Those companies with incremental growth in earnings relative to their revenue growth over time are truly exhibiting *productivity* and *efficiency* with resultant profitability over time. Values of PFT ELS for these companies will be *increasing* while on the other hand, those losing competitive advantages to rivals will exhibit *decreasing* PFT ELS values over time. PFT ELS can provide the investor in Technology stocks with a quantitative dimension to follow these companies with otherwise difficult to comprehend traditional valuation measurements.

Using PFT ELS as a single determinant is unwise. Its movement changes slowly, but over a period of time can point to the company with the best competitive position. In analyzing PFT ELS over time, one might expect that a five-year price appreciation would be linked to the companies with the highest values of PFT ELS and those where the value = > 1.0. However, when analyzing the data by multiple linear regression modeling, there is statistically mild to moderate correlation ($r = 0.45$) of price appreciation at three years rather than five years. Exactly why a five-year financial ratio determinant should have its greatest correlation for three-year positive price appreciation is still being studied. However, one thought may be related to the notion discussed earlier related to a shorter than usual technology business cycles. Further exploration and research is necessary to confirm this preliminary observation or whether non-technology sectors can be evaluated by this methodology.

Author's Disclaimer

Before making any purchase, it is recommended you simply follow the price of the stock over time with its PFT ELS *values and other criterion you deem important before investing. It is very easy to create a shadow portfolio of stocks that you can follow on the Internet at a number of sites before investing. My personal favorite is http//:finance.yahoo.com/ [Portfolios - create]. In addition, every investor should perform their own due diligence in creating a strategy of equity stock selection that meets his/her needs. A good source to view multiple sources of information on news, charts, fundamentals, and other forms of similar investor pattern analysis for a particular stock, can be found on www.onepageresearch.com.*

Chapter 8

Identifying Emerging Tech Trends and Stocks

By James E. Farris, Ed.D.

*If I have seen farther than others, it is because I was standing on
the shoulders of giants.*

-Sir Isaac Newton

Introduction

Many individuals prefer a particular market sector and may choose
to invest in only a few sectors. This is due to a variety of reasons. An
individual may prefer to invest in the sector of their occupation.
Conventional wisdom says it is wise to invest in a market sector where
one has the most knowledge. An auto worker might be more inclined to
invest in the industrial cyclical or transportation sectors because he

knows automobiles and the potential sales for the same. Another individual might prefer to invest in a certain sector due to an interest in the types of stocks in a particular sector. An investor may have a spouse who is taking a prescription drug for a chronic illness or he may have a specific interest in a disease where research about the disease is being conducted by firms in the biotech industry. One's hobbies could be another reason for having an interest in a particular sector. Individuals who are into sports and/or who like to wear current sports apparel might prefer to invest in the leisure market sector.

The technology sector, even though beaten down in 2001, is definitely one of great interest to investors. The economy is being altered faster than any time since the industrial revolution and investors want to know how to select profitable stocks. Most investors are not computer scientists, chip designers, computer specialists or software programmers. Investment analysts tell us that we need to invest in this sector because it means investing in the new economy. The media tells us that technology is bringing new important advances into our daily living. Unfortunately, many analysts have given bad advice in recommending certain technology stocks. The growing e-commerce trend verifies we need to do something, but the question remains, what strategy should we employ when investing in technology companies when one has little, if any, first hand knowledge of the field? A second question, how can we be risk adverse in our investing decisions? In other words, how can we maximize our profits while reducing our risks in a volatile sector with huge price swings? How can we know that we are taking the right path down the technology trail?

The primary goal of this chapter is to help answer these questions. This chapter will present an investment strategy designed to reduce your risk in technology investing, while at the same time give you a methodology you can use to invest in any sector. A second goal is to help you identify a trend or shift in technology in its earliest stages.

We Live in Exciting Times...

One can actually access the new library in Alexandria, Egypt from one's work or home computer. What an amazing time in which to live! Technology and the rapid growth of the Internet and knowledge exchange have made this possible. We live in an era where the knowledge of mankind is doubling roughly every ten years. Unfortunately, not every technology company will survive. As a matter of fact most don't. One of the purposes of this chapter is to help reassure the investor that technology is not dead but rather alive, even though we are experiencing a down turn in the technology business cycle at the time this chapter was written. This chapter will help you identify those technology companies that not only survive but thrive. To help put things in their proper perspective, read the following quote from Suku Ramanthan[42], a noted futurist, technology writer and investor.

> History has shown that we have had at least half a dozen similar transforming "technologies" this century of similar import—electricity, the automobile, vaccines, radio, television, airplanes, spaceships and the Interstate Highway system. In each of the cases, the stock market greatly overestimated the number of companies that would succeed in being leaders in the new "technology". It helped fund a hundred companies for everyone that would eventually make it. In the end, of course, the leaders in each area were only three or four in number. But the stock market had succeeded in its duty of financing the thousands of enterprises from whence the

---

42 Suku Ramanthan, e-mail to *gurus@intrepid.com*, June 2001

Darwinian winners would emerge. One of the interesting items that emerge from reading the press of each era is to see how common the fallacy was that "this time" we have finally succeeded in conquering the business cycle. No more sine waves, no more dips and bumps, just one smooth continuous line going upwards and to the right. In our time, we've had books like "The Long Boom", "Dow 36,000" etc.

I believe that there will always be a business cycle. Human psychology guarantees it. In good times, there is always the tendency to plunge in, take the risk, start the business, invest the money. In bad, the tendency to pull back, to rush to safety, to take the secure job, to clamp down on the wallet.

As an investor, I am interested in the edge conditions, the points of inflection where the curve changes direction. I've never found a way to successfully post good returns at the peak or the bottom of the curve (including never knowing "when" exactly we are at the peak or bottom). At the fulcrum points, very small perturbations make enormous differences in perception. Take the case of a company that is losing five cents a share in times such as now. Because earnings are negative, there is no p/e ratio that can be computed. Because the overall market is depressed, there is often a huge compression of market cap (over 400 companies in tech today are down more than 90% from their highs).

This chapter will help you identify trends and inflection points that will assist you in discovering the technology leaders, regardless of the stage of the economic business cycle.

Identifying Trends in Technology

The previous chapters covered the essentials of fundamental, technical, confirmatory analysis as well as the primary variables and chart patterns to look for when screening for winner stocks. As stated earlier, very few stocks will pass the confirmatory analysis screen and it is quite possible that many market sectors may not have a single stock. The question is how does one select a stock from a particular sector that could be a winner even though it doesn't meet the confirmatory analysis criteria. This chapter will present a template or model that one can use to prospect for technology winner stocks. In addition, this chapter will provide helpful Internet sites and other information resources that have proven valuable in identifying potential winners. Finally, this chapter will help you decide which technology stocks to shadow and invest while reducing your exposure to risk.

Examine Growth to Reduce Risk

Investors, as a group, did not fully appreciate the inherent risks involved in technology investing until the second quarter of 2000. This really hit home to investors during the first two quarters of 2001. The NASDAQ average, where most technology stocks are traded, dropped from just more than 5000 to less than 1700 in less than thirteen months. It became abundantly clear that something was terribly wrong with technology stocks. Investors wanted answers to questions. Why are technology stocks losing momentum? Why are tech stocks experiencing declining share prices? When do you sell or add to your position?

The answer to these question is due to a multitude of factors, such as the bursting of the Internet bubble, cancellation of orders for technology products, inventory buildups, an excessive amount of money spent on Y2K issues, and, a drastic increase in the money supply in anticipation of Y2K shortages, company financing of their products to start up companies that defaulted on their loans, and, the general slowdown in the overall economy which forces companies to spend less on technology. For the individual investor, this is summed up as a slow down in growth. Corporate growth is the fuel for explosive earnings and increased share price. Thus when growth slows, earnings falter and stock prices decline drastically and often with little warning.

Growth at a Reasonable Price (GARP)

In 1997, an investor could throw a dart at a list of technology stocks. More than likely the stock hit by the dart appreciated in price. Now reality has set in and investors have to take a look at the concept of growth at a reasonable price (GARP). What is GARP for a technology stock? If one uses the large cap S&P 500 Index for a base line of growth, one would find a ten-year average growth rate of approximately 10%. Is this reasonable for technology stocks? A quick review of historical investing is important at this point. All new companies grow at a faster rate than older well-established companies and their earnings reflect this trend. Over time, the company matures and growth reverts back to the market average. Wal Mart growth in the 1970's and early 1980's was above the average for the S&P 500 due to opening new stores across the US. The growth of the company slowed in the 1990's when most cities in this country had a Wal Mart and the share price of Wal Mart performed like that of a mature company. Now Wal Mart is again expanding through their new Super Wal Mart and Sam's wholesale discount stores. This has increased their growth as well as their earnings.

Now let's look at a technology company that we have referenced before – Intel. Intel historically has kept a high growth rate by constantly increasing the performance and speed of its microprocessors. About every year, Intel would introduce a newer and faster microprocessor. Hardly a year had passed between the time Intel produced and marketed 300-megahertz chip to when they announced the 400-megahertz chip. The 400-megahertz chip is considered ancient by today's technology standards. One can now purchase a one gigahertz or faster chip. Something has happened to the consumer along the way. The consumer cannot observe either the speed and performance difference between an 800-megahertz chip and that of a one gigahertz chip, and/or he believes that the money he has allocated for technology could best be spent on a new printer or monitor. Thus Intel growth has slowed since box makers are not buying as many chips because consumers are not buying as many home computers.

How does one determine GARP? There is no fixed or one correct answer. At best, it is "one's best guess" determined after using a few simple calculations and basic research. As in most things in life, stay with the simple when doing your calculations. We recommend a simple comparison of the stock under consideration's PE and Price to Sales ratios with that of the S&P 500 Index and the other stocks in the same sector. For example compare the Intel's PE with that of Transmeta and Advanced Micro Devices and then compare the Price to Sales ratio.

Question: *Is Intel's P/E higher or lower than that of the S&P 500 or its competitors?*

Answer: Here is a quick way to find out. Go to *www.onepageresearch.com*. Enter the symbol for the stock under consideration, in our case Intel (INTC). Scroll down to *Guru Analysis*. Click on *Guru Analysis* and look at the opinions of the experts. Do the gurus believe it fair priced, over priced or under priced based on current market conditions and future expectations? There is wisdom in obtaining the opinion of others. Look at the criteria that each of the Gurus uses to select a stock. Note their opinions of current and future revenue growth. Whose opinions do you use and whose do you discard? We suggest going with the majority or with the investment philosophy you most closely identify with and have the most confidence. Since we are looking at growth, review closely Peter Lynch, Martin Zweig and James O'Shaughnessey. Finally, track the stock for at least a quarter preferably two. You might lose some upside potential but you will definitely limit your downside risk.

Stop, Look and Listen

The approach to researching potential technology winner stocks is similar to approaching a railroad crossing. You have to stop what you are doing, be observant and look around you and listen to the winds of change.

First you have to modify the methods you have previously used in researching stocks. In the past, traditional evaluation parameters such as PE were apparently thrown out the window. With the slow down in the economy, investors are interested in PE and GARP again. So what is the novice investor with no technological training to do? You must look around you. The martial art's concept of total awareness of ones surrounding is applicable to technology investing. Observe the landscape. What products are people purchasing, what is being advertised and what are the experts touting? Can you listen to analysts when their job is to sell stocks for their firm? Keep in mind that they often produce good research but have missed the boat in recent times. Can one listen to experts in today's market when their opinions are sometimes contrary to one another? The answer is in part yes and no.

One of the first steps that one can do is to listen to the news. Write down the essential tenets of what is being said about the trends under discussion. If the trend is discussed on a frequent basis, such as on

CNBC, or being reported in magazine stories, then you have a good idea a trend is in the making. Take careful note of analysts' reports or an annual report that mention a trend. When two or more analysts start talking about a trend it is worthy of further investigation. When you read about a recurring theme in articles found in magazines such as *Bloomberg Personal Finance, Wired, Business Week* or *Red Herring*, you should have an idea that a theme is emerging. Can you think of a theme(s) evolving now?

Current Technology Trends

Before you start any adventure into the unknown, you start with what is known and build on the same. The author has identified six current technology trends.

1.   The Internet will disadvantage brick and mortar businesses. Rich media is becoming pervasive. Example: Merrill Lynch starting an on-line investing service.

2.   Reproduction and distribution costs approach zero. Example: Long distance prices are dropping.

3.   Commerce affects or changes shopping patterns and distribution. Example: Wal-Mart adding an Internet business line of goods and services.

4.   Brand name loyalty and authority matter even more in a period of confusion. Example: IBM quality service versus hardware.

5.   Wireless Internet and wireless enabled devices.

6.   VoIP or voice over Internet protocol.

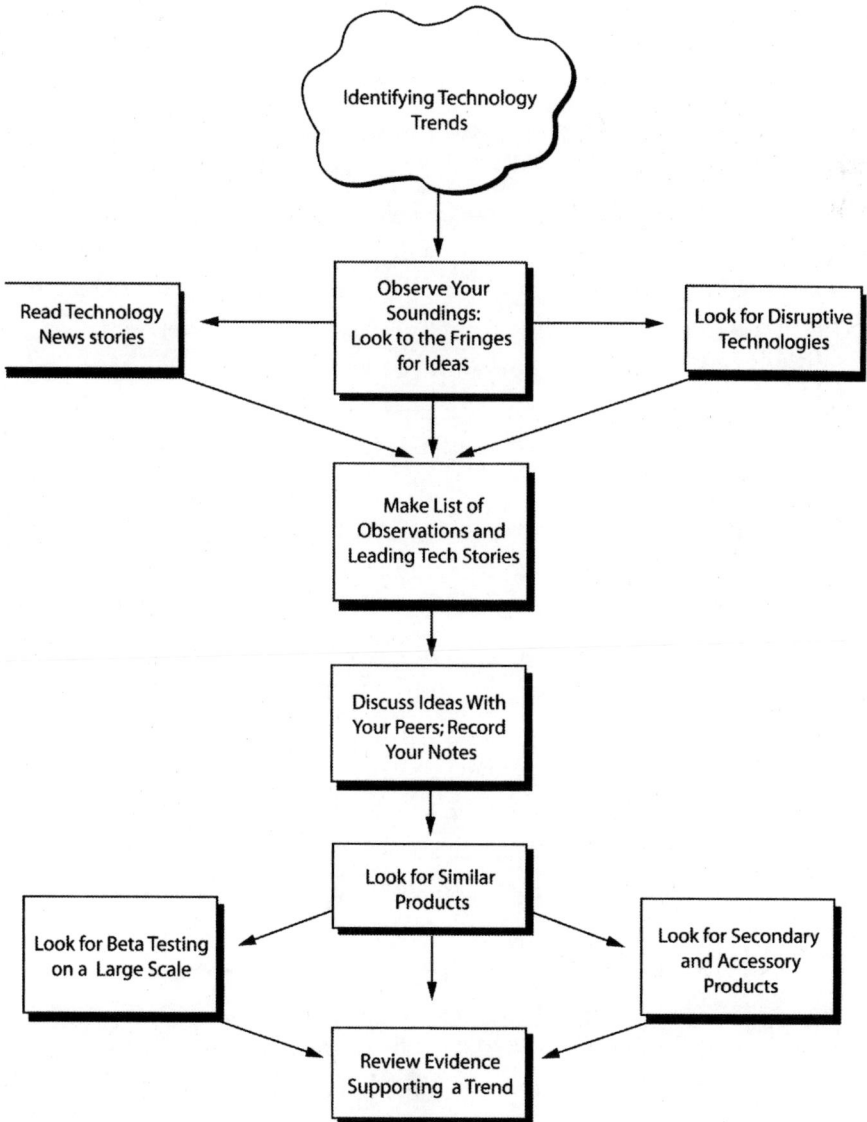

```
                    ╭─────────────────╮
                   (  Identifying Technology )
                   (       Trends            )
                    ╰─────────┬───────╯
                              │
                              ▼
┌──────────────┐      ┌──────────────────┐      ┌──────────────────┐
│ Read Technology │◄───│  Observe Your     │───►│ Look for Disruptive │
│ News stories    │    │  Soundings:       │    │ Technologies        │
└──────────────┘      │  Look to the Fringes│    └──────────────────┘
                      │  for Ideas        │
                      └─────────┬────────┘
                                ▼
                      ┌──────────────────┐
                      │  Make List of     │
                      │  Observations and │
                      │  Leading Tech Stories│
                      └─────────┬────────┘
                                ▼
                      ┌──────────────────┐
                      │  Discuss Ideas With│
                      │  Your Peers; Record│
                      │  Your Notes       │
                      └─────────┬────────┘
                                ▼
                      ┌──────────────────┐
                      │  Look for Similar │
                      │  Products         │
                      └─────────┬────────┘
┌──────────────┐               │               ┌──────────────────┐
│ Look for Beta Testing │◄──────┼──────────►│ Look for Secondary │
│ on a Large Scale      │       ▼            │ and Accessory      │
└──────────────┘      ┌──────────────────┐  │ Products           │
                      │  Review Evidence  │  └──────────────────┘
                      │  Supporting a Trend│
                      └──────────────────┘
```

Discovering New Trends or Shifts in Technology

Discerning a new trend or shift in technology begins by observing what is changing or happening around you. Change, like taxes, is always going to be with us. We have a choice, we can both look for and profit by it or we can allow change to take place and just a wish we had taken action. Have you ever said to yourself, "I wish I had seen the potential for personal computers long before the box makers stocks were selling close to their highs?" What about the rise of e-commerce? Have you noticed that corner mom and pop bookstores are closing their doors because they cannot compete with on-line book retailers?

The best place to observe a battlefield or the landscape is from above or on a high hill. From this perspective you can see the big picture. This is a good analogy for observing the technology landscape. Your first frame of reference should be from afar. You start with the big picture and gradually focus down to the detail. Let's return to the personal computers box makers and use them as an over simplified example. We can observe that individuals are purchasing personal computers and printers and that people are no longer buying typewriters and ribbons. However, we can't observe what is inside the personal computer only the box. In this example, we observe people buying computers but we intuitively know they are buying more than a box. They are in essence purchasing a box containing a hard drive, floppy disk drive, and an assortment of chips and plug in cards. At this level of observation, we are interested only in the fact that people are buying computers and not typewriters.

Look to the fringes for shifts in technology. If there is but one lesson that should be tattooed on our foreheads, it is this: "All interesting movements begin at the fringes." The American War of Independence was started by small bunch of colony politicians, farmers, and tradesmen. The Colonies defeated King George's army. Britain at that time ruled an empire covering one sixth of the earth. Fidel Castro commanded thirty guerrillas when he stormed the Moncada garrison in Cuba. Batista commanded an army of 50,000 soldiers and he ended up fleeing the country.

Companies, like countries, rise and wane. In modern times, Microsoft started as a company of sixteen employees in a single office in Albuquerque and it almost took down IBM in a relatively short time. In the 1950s and 1960s Honda was known as supplier of lawn mowers and motorcycles. Now Honda automobiles outsell General Motors vehicles. General Motors was the world's leading automobile maker during the 1950s and 1960s.

The goal of the investor in identifying trends is to find those companies whose mission is to deliver and manage information to the end use consumer by the least costly and fastest way feasible. Whether it is a service or product, those companies that will be profitable are those who can produce goods and services for the trend while maintaining low fixed costs of operations.

By using the steps mentioned in this chapter and in the previous chapters, you are now ready to begin the journey of technology investing. The place to begin is to examine the underlying themes of technology trends.

Change for the most part starts on the fringes. So if you are observing the battlefield from above, you look to the edges of the battlefield to discover flanking maneuvers of enemy troops. In regards to technology, you look at the fringes as well. Look for those counter cultures or business for ideas. Do you remember who were the first individuals to use the Internet? It was the Department of Defense and university scientists and researchers and not the local retail businesses, brokerage firms or individuals. Looking to the fringes will take some discipline and possibly a shift in how you think. Again, changes will first be noticed at the edge. This is where reading and research comes into play. Make an effort to associate more with the fringe and the people on the fringe than you have in the past.

Disruptive Technologies

Clayton Christensen[43], a professor of business administration at the Harvard Business School, is the author of *The Innovator's Dilemma: When New Technologies Cause Great Firms to Fail.* In his book, Christensen examines companies that were once strong market leaders who lost major market share to companies on the fringes. His research focused on companies that fell from their leadership position due to excessively bad administration while Wall Street was publicly acclaiming the company. A good example is Sears. The management of Sears failed to see the potential that discount retailing would have on their business. In a few short years, a discount store like Wal-Mart became the dominant leader in retailing. Another good example is Digital Equipment. Digital did not realize the impact that the personal computer would have on its bottom line until it was too late. Christensen coined the phase "disruptive technologies" to describe this event.

Disruptive technologies occur whenever the price and/or performance of a company's products and services are more than what the public wants. This situation provides an opportunity for innovative companies to produce cheaper and easier to use products or services for consumers thus displacing the market share of the dominant company. Often the management of the dominant company overlooks the company at the fringe because the products or services offered have lower unit profit margins.

---

43 Clayton Christensen, *The Innovators Dilemma: When New Technologies Cause Great Firms to Fail.* Boston: Harvard Business School Press, 1997

The technology field is ripe for disruptive technologies. At the time this chapter was written, Net2phone and Dialpad.com were obtaining long distance market share from companies like ATT, Sprint and the regional bells. Currently established brokerage companies are threatened by on-line brokerage firms such as E-trade. The take home message for the investor is to look to the fringes for innovative companies that are gaining market shares at the expense of a much larger well-established company.

Develop a System for Retaining Observations

If you observe a change or a potential technology shift, be sure to record what you have seen. If you observe a number of people during your morning commute checking hand-held computers, such as a Palm Pilot, then you should jot down this observation and place it in a file for later review. We suggest you review weekly your file of observational findings. Your observation file should be kept in a manner that is easily retrievable and updated. Items to consider retaining in an observation file are newspaper clippings, magazine articles, promotional advertisements in newspapers, and, personal notes.

Discuss Technology Shifts with Friends Who Share Similar Interests

You should seriously consider setting a side time to have a salon style session each month with a group of individuals who have an interest in discussing trends for investment strategic planning. This can be accomplished via Internet using an on-line chat session, or in person, which is preferable, because the interchange of ideas is easier. Today with a broadband connection to the Internet and a cheap video camera one can even have a face to face video discussion with their friends, which eliminates the need to travel to meetings during bad weather. If at all possible, attempt to have a discussion group of individuals from diverse backgrounds. Don't have all engineers, accountants, computer programmers or physicians, etc., go for a diversified mix and try to include individuals from the fringes. Groups made up of professionals from diverse backgrounds can add insights to a trend that an individual might not observe.

You start by positing a theory to your salon discussion group and observe their reactions. If more than one member of the group makes a statement which validates your theory, you might have identified a trend. If no one agrees with your theory, record the discussion notes and revisit the theory at a future meeting.

The following are some suggested rules for developing a successful salon discussion group.

✓ Ideal group size is between five and ten individuals.

✓ Establish a regular monthly scheduled meeting. Hold the meeting if only two people attend. Use on-line chats if necessary.

✓ Capture the proceedings in some fashion, i.e., notes, recording devices, etc. One member must take the responsibility to send a copy of the main points of discussion to all members regardless on whether or not they attend.

✓ Appoint a group leader and determine a meeting place. The more informal the setting the better it will be. It is also better to meet in a location with minimal distractions such as a member's home. The meeting can be rotated among the member's homes. Having the meeting in a home also provides social interaction in a relaxed setting.

✓ Have assigned readings to keep current of what trends appears to be emerging. A member might suggest a reading a book that follows a technology trend or the leader might assign members to read articles in various technology or application monthly publications.

✓   Have fun. The purpose of the meeting has to have fun while enjoying an intellectually stimulating conversation with the members. This helps to keep the members interested in the subject under discussion and create within them a desire to return to future meetings. Should a member drop out, attempt to replace the member, as you want to keep a core group.

Attempt to Locate the Sources for Technology News

The closer you are to the source the better and more current the information will be. Here again this is where the fringes will become important. Review fringe technology publications. You don't have to be a scientist. You have to be a detective. Look for recurring themes. An excellent source to consult for ideas on the fringes is the Internet. The following are two suggested web sites that can assist you in your research, *www.news.com* and *www.wired.com*.

Search for Tangible Evidence

The next step in the process is to look for tangible evidence that a shift in technology is underway. The key question needing an answer is where does one search for evidence? Start with the broad view of the landscape and then observe from close range. Peter Lynch[44] believed one could find new companies, products and trends by walking into stores and observing the new merchandise that was being stocked and

---

44 Peter Lynch [Former manager of the very successful Fidelity Magellan Fund] author of multiple common sense investing books for the beginning investor.

sold. We suggest that you talk with the sales clerks and store managers to learn how fast the merchandise or services are selling. This will give you and an opportunity to determine which company's merchandise is being displayed. Look at the merchandise and ask yourself, if this is a company that has investment potential. The same principle holds true in discovering trends in technology. For example, if you walked in a Best Buy store and saw cable and DSL modems for sale when last week only 56K modems were available, you would have a good hint that consumers would be purchasing faster broadband modems. Be sure to record your observations.

Another useful method is to review magazines and other sources both on and off line to see if a product or service is being written about on a more frequent basis. For example, if you are seeing more and more advertisements or articles written endorsing a particular product or service, you should take note and see if other publications are also endorsing or describing the product. Look at the editorials and see if a product or a product line is being mentioned on a more frequent basis. Scan several magazines to see if similar advertisements, articles or editorials appear. Look for expert testimony or endorsements regarding a product or service. When you read a product or service endorsement from someone considered an expert in the technology field, then you have a good clue that a trend may be in the making.

Always be looking for evidence of beta testing of a company's product or service on a large scale. A recent example was when a cable television company decided to conduct a large scale beta test of their broadband Internet service. This particular company permitted cable television subscribers to connect for free during the beta test period which brought much attention to their product.

The increased availability of the product or service is another example of tangible evidence. Going back to the cable example, if you heard a local radio or a television commercial promoting fast cable Internet service, you could call your local cable television company to inquire when cable services would be available in your location. You also contact the stores in your local to see if they are demonstrating the service.

Another good evidence indicator would be when one or more companies start selling the same type of product or service. If this is occurring, a trend could be in the making. For example, when the first cell phones appeared, it wasn't long before numerous other companies started advertising their cell phones. The same was true for those companies who provided cellular services. If a product or service is showing up on an ever-increasing basis, then it is likely that a trend is underway.

Be on the look out for secondary and accessory products based on the primary product. For example, when shopping in stores which sell thin client servers, such as Palm Pilots, see if you can observe individuals purchasing secondary products tailored to Palm Pilots. While looking for secondary products, also look for copycat and similar products made by competitors. This is always a good sign since competitors know what is selling and want a share of the market of the new trend.

Finding Outperforming Technology Stocks

Regardless of the sector, one has to initiate a search to find those stocks that are winners.

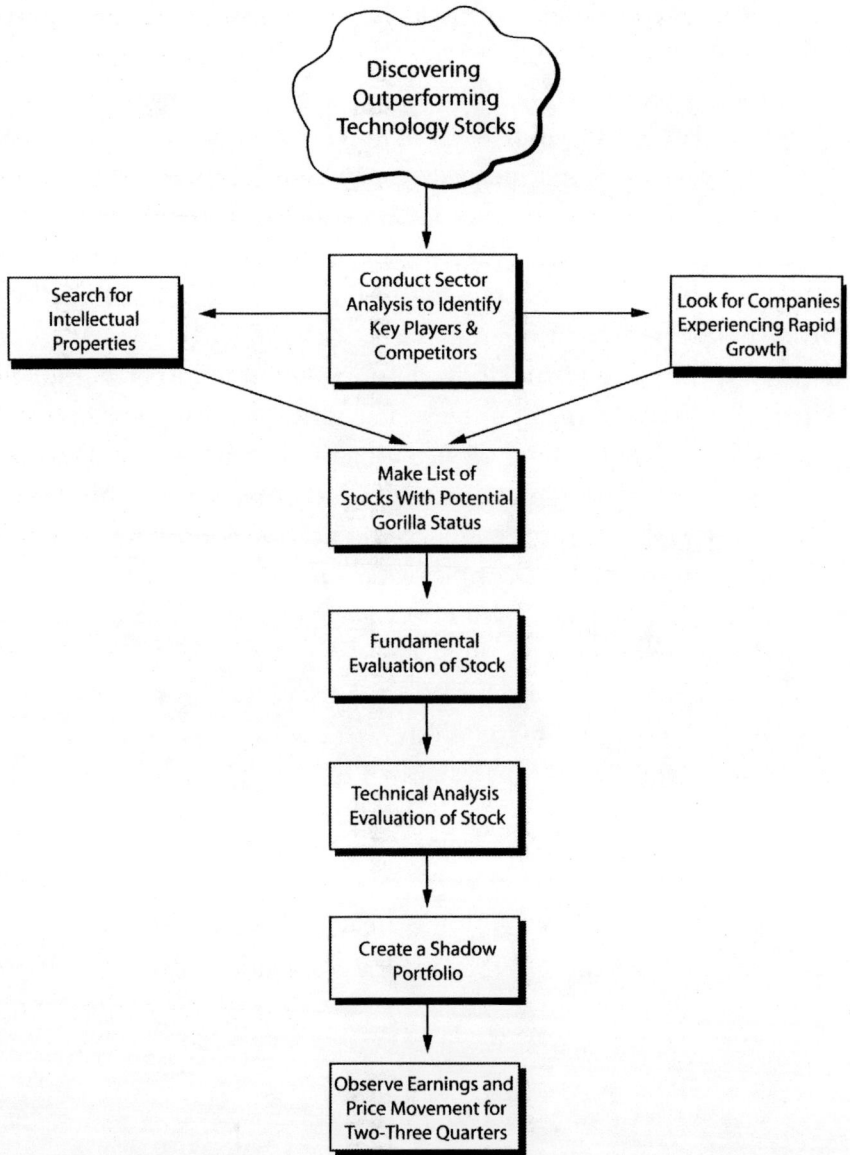

Discovering Outperforming Technology Stocks

Conduct Sector Analysis to Identify Key Players & Competitors

Search for Intellectual Properties

Look for Companies Experiencing Rapid Growth

Make List of Stocks With Potential Gorilla Status

Fundamental Evaluation of Stock

Technical Analysis Evaluation of Stock

Create a Shadow Portfolio

Observe Earnings and Price Movement for Two-Three Quarters

One of the first steps is to identify the leaders in a particular market sector. *The Gorilla Game: Picking Winners in High Technology*[45] is an excellent book on this particular subject. The authors of the book have coined the term "gorilla stocks." A *Gorilla* stock can be defined as a company that holds a market share of one third or greater of a product or service, which has a low-cost structure, high demand for its products or services which enables it to maintain high profitability. Past gorilla stocks include AT&T and General Motors. Gorilla stocks in 2000 include IBM, Microsoft, Wal Mart, Cisco Systems and General Electric. Since gorilla stocks dominate a particular industry, they have a greater tendency to be winners over the long run. Historically gorilla stocks have dominated their particular market sector and have produced better returns than the market in general. The key is to recognize when gorilla stocks start losing their dominate market share and to identify companies that will be the next gorillas.

Sector Analysis and Strategic Mapping: Identifying the Key Players and Their Competitors

(Optional Reading)

It is important to identify those companies that may be involved in the development of a trend. A good site for identifying a company's

---

45 G. Moore, P. Johnson, and T. Kippola, *The Gorilla Game, Picking Winners in High Technology.* New York: Harperbusiness, 1999.

competitors is One Page Research. Go to the *miscellaneous* section and click on *Competitor Analysis.*

The first step in reducing your risk and improving your profits is to identify technology companies that currently possess or have the potential to dominate a particular market or a market segment. This is where competitive mapping becomes important. Transferring quantitative measurement to qualitative scaling enhances one's understanding. The visuals created should help you recognize market leaders more easily than a group of numbers which do not represent anything tangible. Recall the adage about pictures.

Sector analysis and strategic mapping are tools used by analysts to compare and contrast companies in the same field. Traditional sector analysis compares variables such as P/E, Price to Sales ratio (P/S), Beta, Book Value/share, etc. to find the best positioned company. Sector analysis attempts to find the stock with the best P/E, or lowest Price / Book or (P/S) ratio. Strategic mapping uses subjective variables such as the degree of specialization, brand identification, push/pull strategies and distribution channels. The variables used to compare companies and their performance varies from industry to industry. When comparing the retail industry one might use sales per square foot to separate Wal-Mart, K-Mart, Target and Sears from each other. As a way of comparing valuation in the airline sector, you could use passenger revenue per mile flown or cost / per passenger mile flown. Each sector has its own unique parameters that serve to provide a yardstick for comparison.

Another method to perform a sector analysis is to map competitors based on their attributes, which can be quantitative or qualitative or in any combination. Qualitative attributes of the competitors can be placed on each axis thereby combining numerous descriptors of each competitor. The purpose is to produce stratification of the competitors within a specific sector. Construct a graph containing two axes. Let the X-axis be the horizontal line and the Y-axis the vertical line.

Case Study: Domestic Personal Computers (See Figure 3 & 4)

Table 1. Data for Strategic Map (See Figure 3)

PC Maker	Domestic PC Market Share
Dell	17 %
Compaq	16%
Hewlett Packard	12 %
Gateway	9 %
IBM	6 %
E-Machines	2 %
NEC	1 %
Others	37 %
Source: C|Net News.com—Jan. 2001	

Table 2. Data for Strategic Map (See Figure 4)

PC Maker	Consumer Friendliness Rating Ratings: 5 = Best 1 = Poor
Dell	4
Compaq	3
Hewlett-Packard	2.5
Gateway	3.5
IBM	3
E-Machines	2
NEC Packard Bell	1
Source: ZDNet.com —Feb. 2001	

Constructing a Strategic Map in 5 Steps

Using the information from the previous two tables above.

1.   Draw two lines intersecting in the lower left-hand side of the page. Label the axes, let the X-axis represent Consumer Friendliness (a qualitative assessment 5=Best, 1=Poor) and the Y-axis represent Retail PC market share % (quantitative ranking). Examine the percentage market share of the major competitors. The chart shows that Dell is the leader. Using the highest position on the Y-axis, draw a large circle to represent Dell in

the relative position along the X-axis according to consumer friendliness.

2.   Draw those companies in order of rank according to their customer's user-friendliness and adjust the size of the circle in proportion to the market share of each manufacturer.

3.   The size of each circle is based on the market share relative to the leader. In this illustration, Dell and Compaq with near identical size market share are equal and Gateway should be ½ of both Dell and Compaq since its market share is about ½ that of both. Now position each circle (competitor) on the X-axis corresponding to its relative market share and degree of user-friendliness.

Lessons learned from PC Strategic Mapping (See Figure 3 and 4)

Q: Who are the market leaders based on market share and best user friendliness?
A: Dell and Compaq

Q: Who are the largest market share competitors?
A: Dell, Compaq, and Hewlett-Packard

Q: Who are competitors with the smallest market share?
A: E-machines and NEC/Packard Bell

Q: How do they differ from one another?
A: They all have relatively different degrees of consumer friendliness

Q: What do all competitors wish to achieve?
A: Large market share and "Best "Consumer Friendliness

Hint: The arrow connotes where key competitors are setting the direction for others to follow.

The strategic map demonstrates how companies like Dell and Compaq have a large market share while maintaining consumer friendliness. Conversely, IBM would like to move to the upper right-hand quadrant with better consumer friendliness. Once a strategic map has been constructed, additional multiple attributes can be added to understand the differences of each competitor relative to each other.

Researching and Identifying Gorilla Stocks: Ownership of Intellectual Properties

The next step after identifying the key players and their competitors is to research the companies' stories. Look closely for statements or facts demonstrating or explaining why particular companies are the dominant leaders in their sectors. In technology, it is generally a company's intellectual properties, such as patents, which make a particular company a leader. A great source to research for intellectual properties is the narrative or letter to the shareholders. Currently, *www.prars.com* is the best site on the Net. Some companies have their annual report on their web site. An excellent source for examining intellectual properties is *www.delphion.com*. Enter the Company's name and not the stock ticker. This is a great source for investigating and examining a company's patents that have been issued or are pending as well as trademarks. Generally the more intellectual properties the company owns, the greater its chances of becoming a gorilla company or maintaining its gorilla status.

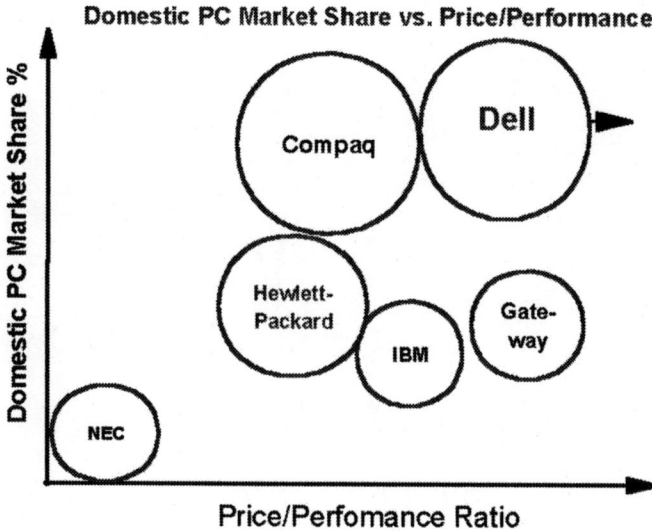

Figure 3. Strategy Map One.

Listen carefully to news regarding a company and read the company's announcements. Also, monitor the announcements and news stories of the company's competitors. If a competitor is gaining market share, it could be due to an intellectual property(s) the competitor owns. Pay careful attention to news pertaining to a company's acquisitions, mergers or partnership arrangements. Gorilla companies buy smaller companies, which possess intellectual properties, which in turn can be leveraged for their benefit. The take home message is the more you understand a company's products, distribution channels, customers and intellectual properties, the better your chances are of selecting potential gorilla stocks while at the same time reducing your investment risk. Sometimes companies have an Achilles heel such as high debt or other factors which can place their Gorilla status at risk.

Retail PC Market Share vs. Consumer Friendliness

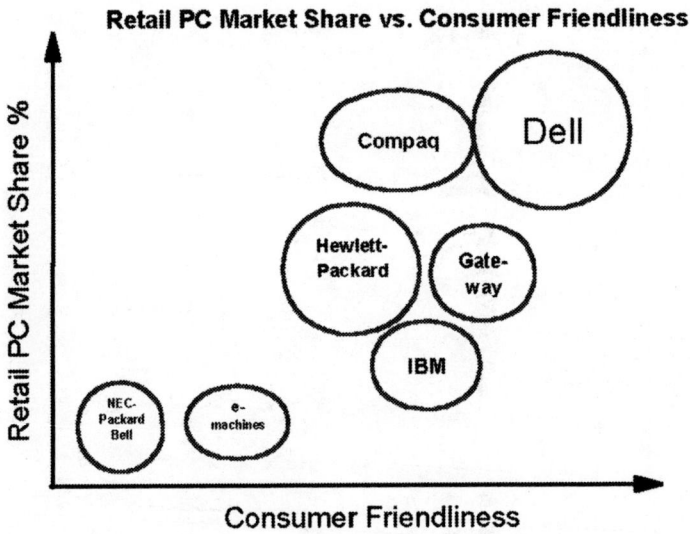

Figure 4. Strategy Map Two.

Closely related to the ownership of intellectual properties is the possession of a technology choke point. Some companies are essential to the expansion and growth of a trend. Companies at the choke point control key components, intellectual properties, source codes, software or other items necessary to make a trend materialize. Companies at the choke point should see increasing expansion in revenues and earnings.

For example, Global Crossing owns the majority of fiber optic cable on the ocean's floor so when a data transmission company wants to deliver data to over seas customers, the company would more than likely use Global Crossing.

Gorilla Companies Grow and Expand

Companies that hold gorilla status are growing and expanding. When growth becomes static and starts declining, then you either have a company that is losing its gorilla status or a company that will never achieve gorilla status unless fundamental changes take place within the company to reverse these trends. Growth is vital. Without growth, corporate earning will not increase and competitors will have an opportunity to increase their market share.

Technology companies grow by either making acquisitions and/or increasing the sales of their product or services. Growing technology companies generally acquire companies which possess technology that will enable them to enhance their products or services lines or increase the synergy of their products. Pay close attention to those companies that are making acquisitions. It is a signal that something is taking place that will affect the future of the company.

The key is to identify those technology companies with increasing growth and increasing growth prospects. What criteria should you look for in a growing company that would make you think that it a gorilla candidate? The answer is in part found through conducting fundamental analysis of the prospective company.

Fundamental Analysis

The primary way of confirming that a technology stock is indeed a gorilla stock or is moving into a position to become a gorilla stock is to submit the stock to fundamental analysis. The fundamental variables and ratios used to identify a potential gorilla technology stock are quite different to the fundamental criteria used in *Confirmatory Analysis*. First, the time frame for reviewing the stock is considerably shorter. *Confirmatory Analysis* examines stocks that have a minimum of five-years of data, which allows an investor to look at stocks from both a growth and value perspective. Five years is much too long when dealing with technology stocks. Changes in technology are rapidly made. The new wired global economy is adapting and embracing new technology very quickly and what is current today is out of date tomorrow. For example, 33 K modems were barely on store shelves when 56 K modems appeared. 486—33-megahertz computers were sold only for a brief time before the introduction of Pentium computers. Furthermore, technology companies are always subject to being purchased by competitors and /or larger companies. What fundamental criteria can an investor use to evaluate a technology stock when technology is changing so fast? We believe there are three variables worthy of consideration in researching technology stocks: a 12 to a 18-months time frame, revenue growth greater than 20% and earning growth greater than 20%.

Since technology changes so fast, the time horizon to look at technology stocks must be compressed. We suggest a 12 to a 18-month time frame. In technology, much can occur in 18 months. However, if no important changes or announcements occur within a technology company, or if the reports coming from the company are static, then there is a good possibility that the company is not making progress in getting its products accepted in the marketplace. On the other hand, if there are frequent positive press releases and news stories regarding the company, take a good look at the stock's revenue and earning growth.

Whenever you can document two or more quarters of accelerating revenue or earning per share (EPS) growth over the last 12 to a 18-months you have a good indication that something positive is happening to a stock. Double-digit revenue and earnings growth are positive signs of company expansion and increasing acceptance of the company's products by consumers. Look for three quarters of incremental 20% or greater revenue growth. A company whose revenues are increasing at this rate is certainly doing something right. This is where some research may be necessary. This information can be found by turning to a company's web page or by calling their Investor Relations department. You can also obtain the company's revenue growth by accessing *One Page Research* and accessing *Fundamental Model Data* under *Company Profile* after entering the ticker symbol.

Technical Analysis

Following fundamental analysis, it is prudent to check the technical trends. Go to *www.bigcharts.com* or one of the other technical chart web sites and enter the ticker symbols of the companies you want to enter.

More than likely, if the stock's fundamentals meet the criteria previously stated then the technicals should reflect an upward trend over the last three-quarters. If the trends are downward or flat for the past 12 to 18 months, continue to monitor the stock for a minimum of three months. If after that time the trends continue flat or downward, look elsewhere for technical stocks to purchase. It would be wise to take a look at the rejected stocks technicals every three months. On the other hand, if the technicals adapt an upward trend, monitor the stock for another two quarters before buying the stock.

Other Factors to Consider in Identifying Gorilla Companies

Look for trends that would lead you to investigate a series of companies. At the time this chapter was written, there was a growing trend for portable computing devices that don't require large drives and meet the basic computing needs of the user. Another trend that appears to be a rave in the music world is the Motion Picture 3 (MP3) web site where one can download the Diamond (DIMD) multiplayer R-10 memory device with CD quality digital sound. These are trends that should lead one to investigate the companies to determine if their revenue and earning growth are increasing each quarter and at what rates.

As a cautionary note, you need to ask if a detected trend is in someway affected by seasonality? Is the possible increase of sales of snow blowers due to heavier snowfalls in the Midwest or is it due to the increasing popularity of snow blowers? Another example, is the increase in the sale of greeting cards due to Mother's Day or an increase in sales of greeting cards in general. To help you answer the seasonality question, examine the increasing sales and revenue growth for two or more consecutive quarters.

Other places to look for clues in identifying gorilla companies are trade publications. See if the trade publications are mentioning the products on an ever-increasing basis. This is subjective, but often-subjective observations can be one of your best clues. If the product appears in editorials, testimonials, or commercials in *Red Herring,*

Wired, Bloomberg's or any of the other trade magazines, then you have a solid clue that the product or service is getting ever increasing acceptance by the marketplace.

How to Identify Web Based Gorilla Companies

Although web based companies are not considered in the truest since technology companies, they do rely on technology to sell their products or services. How does one identify a potential web-based gorilla company? In addition to the traditional methods discussed in other chapters, other variables should be taken into consideration. One variable is the number of subscribers or members a web site has and the popularity of the site. The popularity status can be observed by looking at the number and type of companies who place advertisements on a site and the amount of money the advertisers spend. Another factor is the amount of time an individual spends on a site. These factors are good indicators of a growing web-based company that has the potential to become a gorilla. A good site to check the aforementioned indicators is *www.mediametrics.com.*

Another method idea worthy of consideration is to take the total revenues for a quarter and the total customer base and dividing one by the other. Do a little back tracking and see if the revenues per customer are increasing or decreasing. If the revenues continue increasing, you might have found a web-based gorilla company.

Create a Shadow Portfolio

A shadow portfolio is a simulated portfolio of stocks, which can be used by an individual without any outlay of capital. It is always advisable to develop a shadow portfolio of stocks to see how they are progressing before you make a purchase. One of the best sites to establish a shadow portfolio is *http://quote.yahoo.com/* under portfolios. Create a shadow portfolio of identified stocks and observe them for one to two quarters. This should be sufficient time to determine if something is a trend that will last or if it is a fad.

While following the shadow stock's performance more than two or more quarters, be sure to look at the company's fundamentals and chart patterns. Look for those chart patterns in your shadow stocks that are definitely trending upward. The bells should really be sounding loudly when an upward chart movement is followed by two or more consecutive quarters of increased earnings. If you can see a trend upwards over the past two quarters, then you can have a higher degree of confidence that your stocks are on the right track. Remember to use both fundamental and technical tools to help you select potential winners.

The next step is to invest money on a dollar cost basis into a basket of identified stocks that have both good fundamental variables and technical patterns. After you make your investment, continue to track the stocks and be prepared to exit those stocks that over time appear to lose their earning and revenue growth momentum or whose technicals go flat or start trending downward. Reinvest the money obtained from the sale of loser stocks by adding to your position in those stocks which continue to pass the test of time and still receives favorable reports from analysts.

Conclusion

If you use the ideas and suggestions in this chapter, you can create a strategy that will allow you to purchase technology stocks that over time should be financially rewarding while at the same time lowering your investment risk. There is a high probability that you will select gorilla stocks based on quantitative variables and not on rumors or speculation. Always put the odds in your favor. Make it your goal to invest in a basket of technology stocks and avoid making gambling decisions. Once you purchase a technology stock be sure to continuously monitor the stock. Review the news regarding the company and always keep in mind that much can happen in the technology field in just a short time. Always look to the fringes for ideas. Remember to do your research and due diligence.

Chapter 9

Stock Screening & Confirmatory Analysis®

By Richard J. Davis, M.D., M.B.A.

I am not a victim,
I am a survivor.

-Lance Armstrong, three time winner of the Tour de France

Introduction

It has always been more than half the battle in researching stocks to winnow the vast universe of over 8,000 listed and publicly traded companies to a small number from which to perform due diligence. Resources about researching individual stocks were mostly confined to reading brokerage analysts' opinions or taking a trip to the public library to read *Value Line*® on a Saturday afternoon, copying copious notes about specifics of each company. Of course the Internet placed voluminous information at the feet of the individual investor, but it was overwhelming as to specific content for use. Learning foundations of stock screening to find stocks with strong fundamentals and technical patterns has been the goal of this book. However, with many financial web sites, the individual investor has been empowered with numerous web sites to perform stock screening according to his / her own criteria. Rapid shifts in the market occur from momentum (growth) to value (worth) and into different sectors of the market. In this chapter, I will introduce the reader to my favorite web sites for stock screening on the Net and assist the reader with additional criteria where to find specific stocks favoring value, growth and other criteria.

Using Our Website's Fundamental Model Preset Screening Criteria

From our home page, *www.confirmatoryanalysis.com*, you will find a button for *stock screening* already defaulted to three of our major fundamental model criteria. This will immediately yield a list of stocks with Fundamental Model scores equal or greater than 75 points of about 100 or so stocks. Now add additional criteria from our fundamental model with values for each parameter we feel are threshold ones. You will continually filter down the number of stocks to a mere handful as you approach one hundred points. All will possess strong fundamentals, but not all will have stellar price charts trending upwards. I would recommend evaluating twenty-five to fifty stocks initially whose fundamental scores are greater than seventy-five, but less than ninety points. Clicking on the symbol will take to an area where a price chart is readily available for you to decide if the stock is going up, going down, or sideways? Remember Chapter 2? As an additional exercise, the reader is encouraged to vary threshold values in the major areas we have set as our default criteria. Loosening the threshold criteria for our default values will dramatically increase your number of stocks to evaluate. Conversely, increasing the default values will reduce the number of stocks passing your filter. Always work with a manageable number of stocks to find a couple for your due diligence. After identification, completely investigate and analyze your short list completely to your satisfaction to determine if the stock fits your own investment needs. Watch your stocks in a shadow portfolio to be sure their price charts continue going up before making an investment decision of adding to your portfolio.

In the spring / summer 2001, finding technology stock prices going up was almost impossible. Constant worries of valuation with P/E in excess of 100 were common as reduced earnings produced falling prices. In terms of sales and earnings, these great growth companies continued to claim failure in " earnings and revenue visibility, " thus making them expensive stocks to own with very high P/E ratios since the " E " was shrinking. As you recall from earlier in this book, our fundamental model uses a balance between growth and value. However, with growth less favored by the overall market, looking elsewhere and creating different models based on differing weighting for value and growth may be the best choice for finding potential stocks to either shadow or purchase. As you are reading through these sections, think of stock screening like a coffee filter. You don't want to drink your coffee with the grounds in the cup.

Very Basic Stock Screening…www.stockscreener.com

If you are looking for a ground zero approach to stock screening, i.e., the " Joe Friday[46] "approach to stock screening, then this web site may be on your beat. Assume for a second, *growth* stocks are out of favor, and *value* stocks are in vogue. To find *value* stocks using one radio button enter your choice for market size[47], i.e., Small-Cap, Medium-Cap or

[46] Joe Friday was the main character in one of the first TV police dramas called *Dragnet*. His style of investigation when questioning witnesses was always *"…just the facts, ma'am!"*

[47] Small Capitalization stocks are usually less than 500 MM, Mid-Caps 500 MM-1 billion, and Large Caps greater than 1 billion.

Large-Capitalization stocks, and the appropriate criterion for each category will be preselected. You're ready to screen by hitting the Go button! Screening for value stock using this methodology will look for fundamentals *below* the current market multiples in each of the following categories:

✓   P/E (< 15—20)
✓   P/Sales or Revenue (< 2.0—2.5)
✓   P/Book (< 2)
✓   Debt/Equity (< 100)
✓   Current Ratio (0.6—2.0) depending upon market capitalization, these ranges will vary.

Conversely, let's say *value* stocks are now out of favor in a market lead by stocks with significant growth. Once again on *www.stockscreener.com*, select find *growth* and input your choice of market cap stock desired and you are ready to screen for *growth* stocks according to the segment, i.e., capitalization specified portion of the stock market. Common characteristics of *growth* stocks will be the following:

✓   High P/E's relative to the market multiple
✓   5-Yr Earnings Growth in Mid-Cap/Large-Cap stocks
✓   High 1-Yr Earnings Growth
✓   High1- Yr Revenue Growth
✓   Low Debt/Equity in the small cap segment.

Choosing Stock Sectors for Growth and Value Stocks

Before choosing a market segment, i.e., Small-Cap, Mid-Cap, Large-Cap of the overall market to identify which segments are in short-term or long-term uptrends.Go to One Page Research, and enter the following symbols to bring up the default three-month chart of the underlying indices:

S&P Small Cap 600	^SML
S&P Mid-Cap 400	^MID
S&P 100 Index	^OEX

Visually look at the chart and ask yourself what you have learned from Allan Harris about technical analysis. Is the index going up, down, or sideways? Go to additional charts and select 1 year. Again ask yourself about the overall trend. This should provide the reader with determining not only the overall direction of the market segment, but which segment to *screen* for *growth* or *value*. In fall 2000 and early summer 2001, *growth* stocks in the S&P Mid-Cap 400 were outperforming the overall market, i.e., S&P 500.

An often overlooked category in today's investing theses and strategies are high-yield stocks. Those stocks with high dividend yields are commonly overlooked. The reason for avoidance is due to the fact high-dividend yielding stocks usually have relatively low price appreciation over time. In addition, any dividend is taxed at the investor's highest marginal rate.

In summary, this is an excellent site to begin developing techniques of stock screening. It provides nice preset values for overall growth and value parameters and allows the reader to select the market segment for screening as well. Don't forget once the stock is selected, apply Confirmatory Analysis principles in your quest for finding potential winning stocks.

Next Best Thing to Being There...www.quicken.com

Under the Investing Tab on the home page *Stock Screener* listed is *Finding New Ideas*. If you chose the *Popular Search* category, it is similar to the site discussed above. If unsure which criteria you are looking for in stock screening, then choosing the *Easy Search* category will guide your efforts, step-by-step. Starting with a desired sector, you are prompted for market capitalization, specific valuation criteria, common growth rates in terms of EPS and REVS, and finally, price per share. This screen is very good for those who like prompting for each step in building their own fundamental model.

Summing up, perhaps the most familiar stock screening search on Quicken.com is the *Full Search* option. Presets for Confirmatory Analysis's basic Fundamental Model utilizes this great resource since it can be customized to narrow down further a long list of potentially promising stocks. This site is so easy to use it could easily be your default for stock screening on the Net for those wishing to specify all criteria in performing stock screening from ground zero.

Looking for Advanced Stock Screening...try www.marketguide.com

Access from the home page under *Screening Tools* along the left-side of the home page. Using Net Screen from *www.marketguide.com* can be time consuming, but rewarding. A timely database updated frequently is clearly a big plus. Unfortunately, there is clearly a learning curve before using this site effectively. Fortunately, the well-written tutorials [Learn to use NetScreener]on the web site for customized stock screening makes this more than a fifteen minute exercise. However, you are rewarded for your effort by some of the best custom stock screening available on the Internet. Although not intuitive, you might wish to wait until a rainy day before tackling this site and gaining mastery.

In summary, with all that said and done, this is one of the most powerful sites available to customize, save your custom stock screens, and download to a spreadsheet. Once you learn this stock screening on this site, you may never go elsewhere finding stocks fulfilling criteria which meet your expectations for either adding or constructing stock portfolios to shadow or create for ownership.

Honorable Mention Category...Microsoft's Money Central Investor

Why honorable mention you ask? Well this is not an easy link to find, but truly a hidden jewel and worth the effort once you have created a bookmark for *Microsoft's Money Central Investor*. You will find it only works in ActiveX capable browsers such Microsoft Internet Explorer Browser (IE 5.0 or greater). Using Microsoft Internet Explorer, find *www.moneycentral.com*, click on the *Investing tab*, then *Stock Screener* under in the *Stock* category located on the left side of the page. Find *Custom Search* and you are greeted with prompts and easy-to-use pull down menus for criteria to screen. Note: You may be prompted to download a small application for this to work properly. Do so since installation is snap for this plug-in. This sets a cookie in your browser to recognize the site when you return to it later. Custom parameters can be easily inputted creating a equally powerful search engine for stock screening as its advanced counter part on *www.marketguide.com*.

In summary, Microsoft Money Central is hard to find, but once set up add to your favorites in IE so you can readily retrieve at any time in the future. Its strong suit is the intuitive interface allowing screening criterion to change on the fly. In addition, a great portfolio tracker function elsewhere on the site makes your efforts even more worthwhile effort.

Stock Screening Pitfalls...and How to Avoid Them

With the ease of on line Internet stock screening tools, it is easy to think of them as *black box* strategies for investing. Alternatively, they can be a great place to start your own personal data mining for prospective stocks to watch or add to your portfolio. If you have run screens on one or more of the stock screening sites above, you will find results differ. Why do similar criteria on different sites' yield different lists of stocks passing the same screen? If we look at the common explanations of this problem, then it becomes apparent that *one* or *more* of the following issues are the cause of the discrepancy:

✓   *Sites use different databases and update them at different intervals*
✓   *Blind spots in selecting inappropriate screening parameter for a sector, i.e., low P/E's for high growth technology companies*
✓   *Screening was used as the last step in stock selection*
✓   *Use of stock screening for solely technical criteria such as price action and volume rather than fundamental criteria*
✓   *Failure of performing investor due diligence*
✓   *Reliance on using out-dated criteria, i.e., those not currently valued by the market for price performance and appreciation*

Conclusion

In this chapter, I have supplied the reader with the most current and best available web sites available for stock screening. Ranking them by ease of use and functionality, *www.quicken.com* is probably the easiest and most versatile to use for the beginning to intermediate investor. Once an individual becomes proficient and is comfortable with the explanations of goals behind growth, value, momentum, etc., then moving to the more sophisticated screens such as *www.marketguide.com* and *Microsoft's Money Central's Investor* screener becomes a natural progression as the investor becomes experienced.

Finally, an important point to note is once a list of potential stocks has been created, sorting down to acceptable numbers such as 20-25 stocks is a mandate for efficient use of time. In our final chapter, we will assist the reader in performing *due diligence* by walking them through using One Page Research as one of the easiest ways to accomplish this goal.

Chapter 10

One Page Research® —Probing a Company

By Richard J. Davis, M.D., M.B.A.

The ability to ask the right question is more than half the battle of finding the answer.

-*Thomas J Watson, Sr.*
Founder , IBM

Introduction

The individual investor is faced with many challenges when researching a stock. First, and foremost, where should I go? What should I read? What numbers are important in defining whether or not a stock is worthy of purchase and addition to an investment portfolio geared for holding longer than a few minutes or hours. Second, once information is obtained, what does it mean, or does this mean good or bad things for a company's stock?

Hopefully, the focus of the antecedent chapters has been to set the stage for using One Page Research. The authors have attempted to weave a tapestry of their understanding and experience using fundamental and technical analysis, establishing Confirmatory Analysis as a tool for selecting stocks. This chapter will furnish one view of performing due diligence that is used by the authors. Certainly, many other methods are appropriate. However, I will take you on a tour creating a methodology for probing stocks that uses One Page Research. This tool will optimize your effort and minimize your time needed to use the tools and knowledge gained in the previous chapters of this book.

Authors Note:

When using One Page Research, a broadband connection works best, but a dial up connection will suffice. Linked web pages and servers may be down or slow during periods of Net congestion. Every attempt is made to keep the links current and the information coming to you from the best sources possible.

Onepageresearch.com…Quick Scan

Medicine, like many other disciplines of science, often requires rapid assessment for making a diagnosis. A physician cannot treat until he/she has a diagnosis in hand for which to prescribe medication or recommend surgery for a patient when appropriate. One Page Research (See Fig 1) is one place where rapid assessment, using a minimal investment of time to collect all the key variables necessary for stock evaluation, can occur with the input of a single stock ticker symbol.

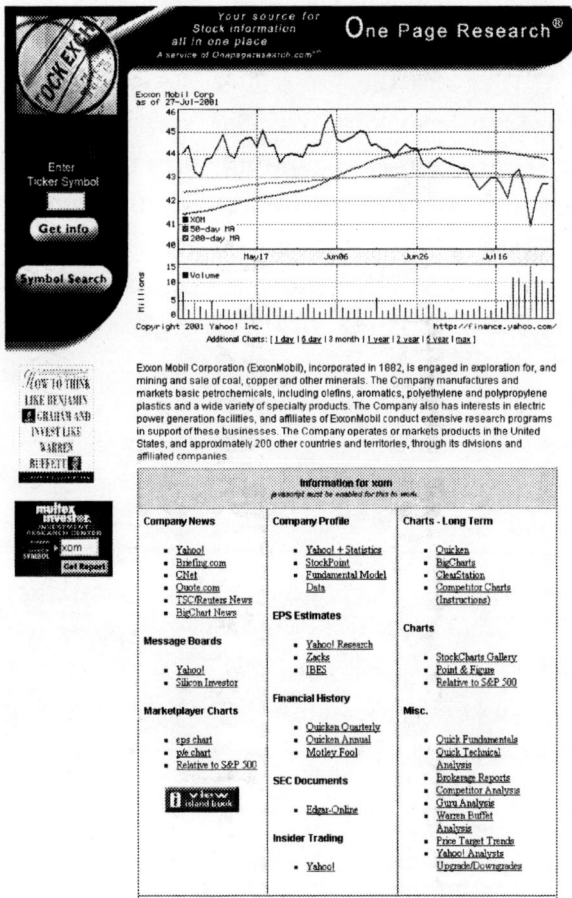

Figure 1. OnePageResearch.com

By now, you may have been to *www.onepageresearch.com* many times. However, if you are going there for the first time, it may have a slightly different appearance due to updated links and categories. Let's use what I call a *Quick Scan* (See Figure 2) approach.

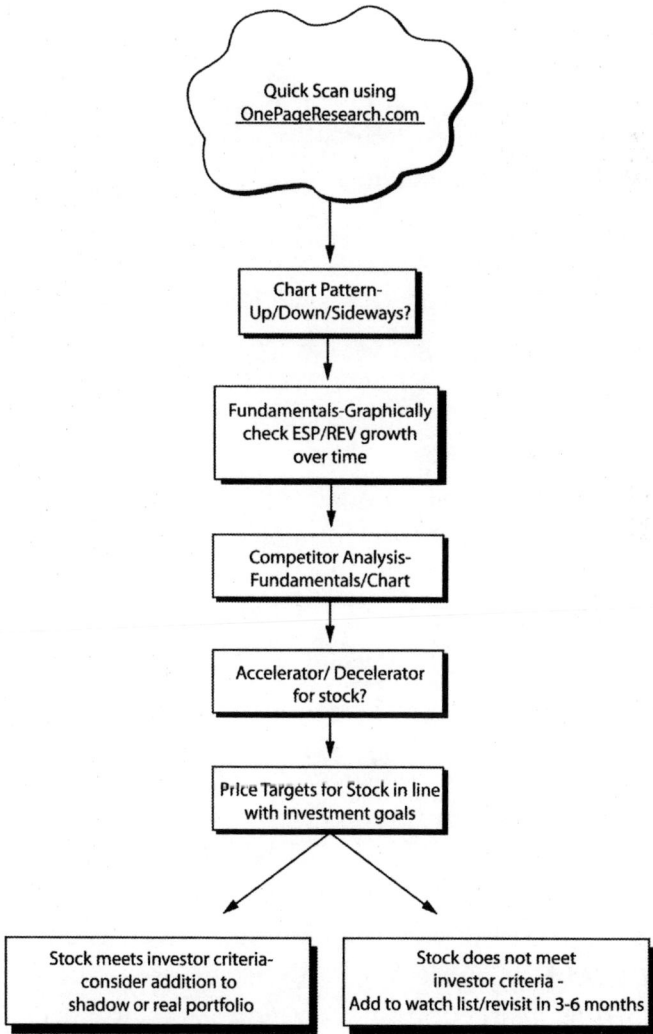

Figure 2. Quick Scan

Chart Pattern—Up/Down/Sideways?

Use Allan Harris's three second visual test: Is the stock going *up*? Can you make this assessment from the three-month default graph on the home page of One Page Research? Short term trends will show the stock trading above its 50-day moving average and longer term above the 200-day moving average depicted on the default chart. If the trend is not readily discernible, then check either 2, 5-year or max from the main chart to secure a longer view via *Additional Charts.* More charting resources can also be found at *Charts-Long Term* or in *Charts.* Another nice Technical Analysis methodology is Point and Figure Analysis. Unfortunately, this is beyond the scope of this book, but useful information on the site can route to *Instructions* on the linked site. What appears next is a three-month price chart (short-term) of the stock as the default charting mode with fifty (50) and two hundred (200) day moving averages displayed. Visually use the three-second rule of Allan Harris. Is the stock going up, down or sideways? If uncertain or it appears like sideways price movement, then use longer time interval charts to answer the question satisfactorily.

Fundamentals—Graphical Depiction

If you have already completed stock screening using our fundamental calculators or by one of the methods described in Chapter 9, then this step will only serve as second opinion to nicely show up trends in both long term EPS and REV growth. If you are researching a single stock, follow the instructions in Chapter 5's graphical depiction for 5-Yr EPS/REV Growth (See Chapter 5, Figure 3). Other fundamental criteria for viewing data for the stock being researched are easily found in the *Fundamental Model Data* under *Company Profile* on One Page Research. Quick scanning of those parameters as discussed in Chapter 3 and 4 will greatly assist answering the key question, is this a stock with *strong* fundamentals?

Competitor Chart Analysis and Performance Against S&P 500 Index Benchmark

Comparing competitors with their respective price performance charts is a good way to determine if you are finding the strongest stock in the sector you are researching (See Figure 3). If you click on *Competitor Charts* under *Charts-Long Term,* you can select stocks to compare on their relative price performance to the one you are currently evaluating. Sometimes a competitor will be outperforming the stock you are researching and taking a step back to review the competitor's fundamentals is worth doing. Since you want stocks in sectors you are selecting to be leadership companies, this often provides a *big picture* view for investors. Creating too many competitors' charts just doesn't make sense since it is hard to discern more than five at a time to find the one or two leaders. When multiple competitors are present, graph groups of five, and select the top two or three, and then continue working down the list until all competitors have been evaluated. These instructions are also under *Competitors Charts* on One Page Research.

Competitors Charting using
OnePageResearch.com
Charts-Long Term
Click on Competitor Charts

Select no more than
4 competitors

Hit Compare and
view chart patterns

Identify strongest chart patterns;
repeat selection until top 3
competitors remain

Researched Stock in
final 3 strong charts?

Stronger
performance by
another Competitor?

Competitor chart
analysis complete

Consider
Competitor
vs.
Researched
Stock

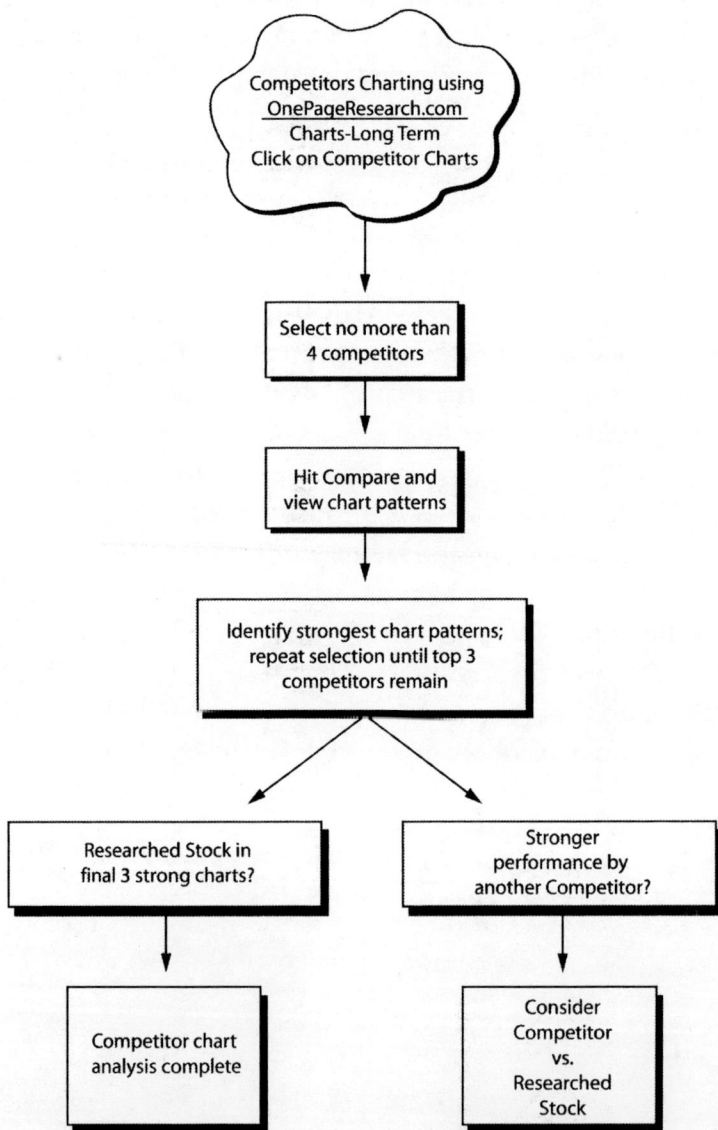

Figure 3. Competitor Charting

Another benchmark, when evaluating price performance via its chart should compare the stock's relative price appreciation to the S&P 500 Index over the same time interval. On One Page Research, by clicking on Relative to the S&P 500, a rapid comparison is possible. Although comparing stocks to a benchmark such as the S&P 500 was not covered in great detail in this book, it remains the default gauge by which professional money managers, mutual funds and institutions compare their effectiveness, and by which their compensation and bonuses are linked. You should think of yourself as head of your own mutual fund of stocks and justify any purchase of a stock underperforming the S&P 500 Index.

Fundamental Analysis of Competitors

Finding a stock worthy of your hard-earned investment dollars is a challenging task. As you continue your due diligence, I recommend performing a competitor analysis for fundamentals of your stock and its competitors. Certainly, your stock may be a star, however, there may be another stock with better prospects or improving fundamentals than the one you have selected. On One Page Research (See Figure 4), click on Competitor Analysis under the Misc. portion of the page. You will see the key competitors listed under Competitive Analysis on the linked site. If you wish to rank order or sort by various fundamental criteria such as 5-Yr Earnings Growth, or ROE, then scroll down the choices in Rank by section of the linked page. Instantly, the rank order of the criteria enables you to visually see the competitors by your selected relative criteria. You also can scroll down and scan the page seeing how each key competitor compares to your stock solely by the numbers. After completing this step, ask yourself, how does your stock compare on the fundamentals?

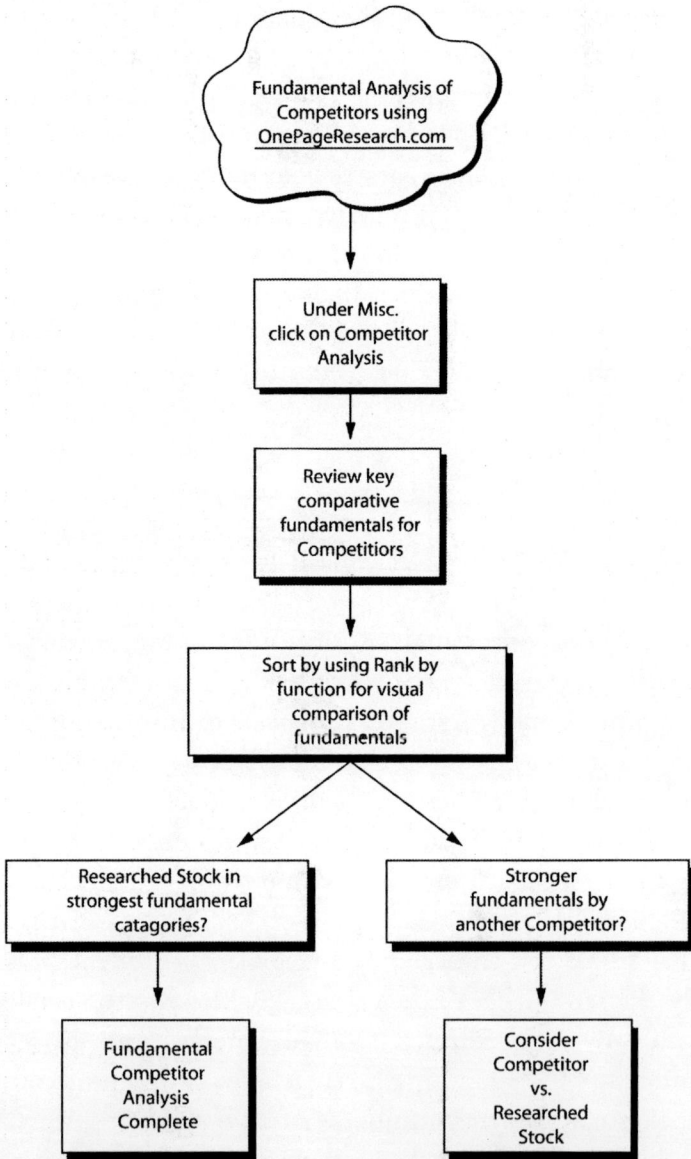

Figure 4. Fundamental Analysis of Competitors

Accelerators/Decelerators Which Affect Stocks

It is always prudent to check the news about a company, going back at least three months or more if possible. However, if your stock screening for example, yields a tobacco stock, then the issues of industry liability may be a difficult issue to factor into a stock's value or potential price appreciation going forward. It is often said that a stock's price has all the good and bad news already factored into it at any given moment. This is partially true since we are dealing with an efficient market where pricing inefficiencies are uncommon. If a company forecasts a shortfall in revenues or earnings for the current quarter or next, the market reacts swiftly, and the stock's price can move rapidly up or down. Another issue that is hard to assess from Company News on One Page Research may be pending or present intellectual property infringements. These usually are in the area of trademark disputes or patent infringement issues. They usually mean legal expenses, either way as plaintiff or defendant. Both are expensive to the company with the outcome unpredictable. A call to a company's investor relations about any pending litigation may be an inexpensive way to answer this question if any doubt exists.

On the positive side, good news regarding better than expected earnings, revenue growth, important product releases, or strategic partnerships can signal improving stock prices in the short term. Factoring long-term sustainable competitive position from these issues is more difficult.

Other catalysts which may affect a company's stock are trends in the macroeconomic environment for product demand and dominance. The reader is referred to the discussion in Chapter 8 for identifying choke points, where competition and market dominance can be seized. Investors' perceptions are often much higher for a perceived trend than any company can deliver. For example, major themes can often trigger a run up in stock prices before a product or service is released. Take for example the area of biotechnology test kits for disease, diagnosis or treatment response. Innovative technology can produce tectonic shifts in traditional business or consumer behavior. Examples are B2B (Business-to-Business) or B2C (Business-to-Consumer) Internet companies or online grocers with home delivery (freeing the consumer from the need to go to the grocery store). Looking at the rise and fall of these companies clearly reflects the expectation or hype often factored into the stock price. However, successful execution of the company's business plan may be years away from profitability, and assuming everything will proceed on track as stated in the pro forma for five years in the future. Many of these so-called story stocks may trade at multiples in hundreds of either revenues or earnings. You will find no such traditional valuation models for these companies, but individual investors should have deep faith in the business plan and hopeful execution. This group of stocks may have wonderfully up trending charts, but no tangible fundamental basis for competitive advantage or long-term profitability.

An additional category that often changes the course of stocks is management. Companies whose boards bring about a new CEO from another successful company often have their stock moved upward. Conversely, illness, injury or other losses of senior management in an otherwise successful company can create volatile stocks prices.

Message Boards may produce hours of interesting reading about a company, but rarely information that would be considered insider information, which would be illegal. However, unless you know the individual personally, his/her information should be taken with a cautious eye of skepticism. Conversely, one can sometimes find an answer to nagging questions about a company, product or competitor, by posting a query and assessing the reply for veracity.

Company News on One Page Research lists some of the authors' perceived best sources for researching current/past news for an individual company. Readers will find some duplication of material carried by each source, but will ultimately find one or two sources they find most informative. Over time, the reader will rely upon these sites for accurate and unbiased reporting and information.

Setting Goals or Price Targets....

In any case, investor perceptions about an industry, sector and company future can change rapidly. Watching the stock carefully and setting price targets for appreciation completes the cycle of identifying stocks worthy of addition to your portfolio, but more importantly realizing profits from taking the risk of ownership. Many shrewd investors claim you should have a price for selling a stock on the day it is purchased. For the individual investor, this is a hard target to establish. We will discuss where to find such a possible long term twelve-month target using One Page Research.

If you have a ceiling for profits to soar to, then you must have a floor to preserve capital. If your stock fails by eight to ten percent, then some informed investors recommend selling to prevent further loss. During extreme market volatility or news, your loss would be capped. Each individual investor must decide their own threshold of risk in purchasing equities.

Analysts Twelve Month Price Targets...

To determine what analysts think are twelve-month price targets for a stock. (See Figure5). Here is what sell side analysts believe are the upside targets for your stock under research. The hardest question to answer is whether or not this an acceptable upside reward to take versus the risk of a possible ten percent loss or more? One way to minimize risk is to avoid purchase when the current price is close to the projected twelve-month price target. Often analysts lower equity recommendations as soon as a stock hits their price targets, thus lowering investor expectations, and selling occurs. By the same token, the same analysts might raise their price targets if a particular company was performing well above expectations. It is beyond the scope of the present book to produce an extended discussion of determining reward versus risk based on chart price patterns because this is very unpredictable science and difficult to replicate.

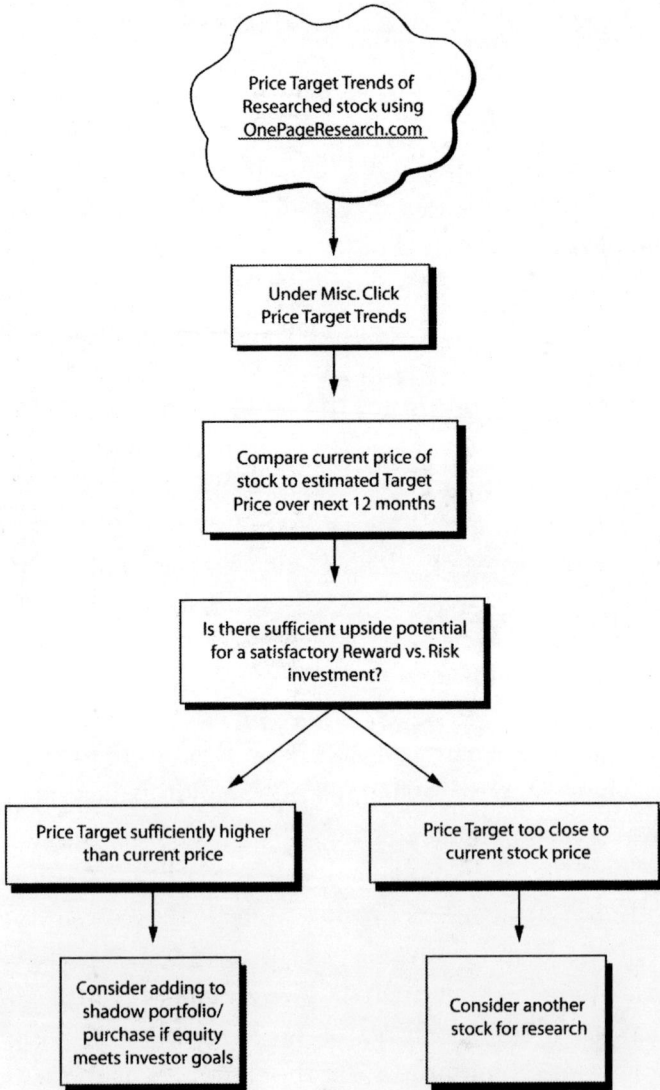

Figure 5. Price Target Trends

Due Diligence is done... What Next?

Congratulations! You have performed all the necessary steps to make a decision about a stock. Should you buy it now before it goes up more or wait to be sure by placing in a shadow portfolio. Admittedly, this is always the most agonizing decision time for investors. Although I don't have any certain rules for investors, consider the following. If you have identified a stock with strong fundamentals, going up in price in a down market, then realize your stock is outperforming most other stocks. Conversely, if your stock is underperforming the overall market, then revisiting it later in 3-6 months to see if it is outperforming the market will be soon enough. Making long term decisions using Confirmatory Analysis to find winning stocks is both an art and science.

How Does My Stock Rank Among Experts... Guru Analysis

(Optional Reading)

After you have completed your own due diligence and have found a potential winning stock, there remains one optional step to consider. In my opinion, this fun step looks at how other noted famed gurus of the investment world might view your personal stock selection.

Most noted investors with celebrity status such as Peter Lynch, James O'Shagnessey, David Dreman, Martin Zweig, William O'Neil, Kenneth Fisher, and the fabled Warren Buffett have their own special strategies for stock selection. It is very interesting to see how they would gauge your stock viewed through their glasses. Does it pass their criterion? Is there some reason that it doesn't pass their scrutiny? All gurus in this league freely admit to their own failures in stock selection, i.e., a stock declines despite careful research and due diligence by the experts before purchase. It happens to everyone, and most are humbled indeed, ready and willing to discuss why their methods failed with a particular stock or company.

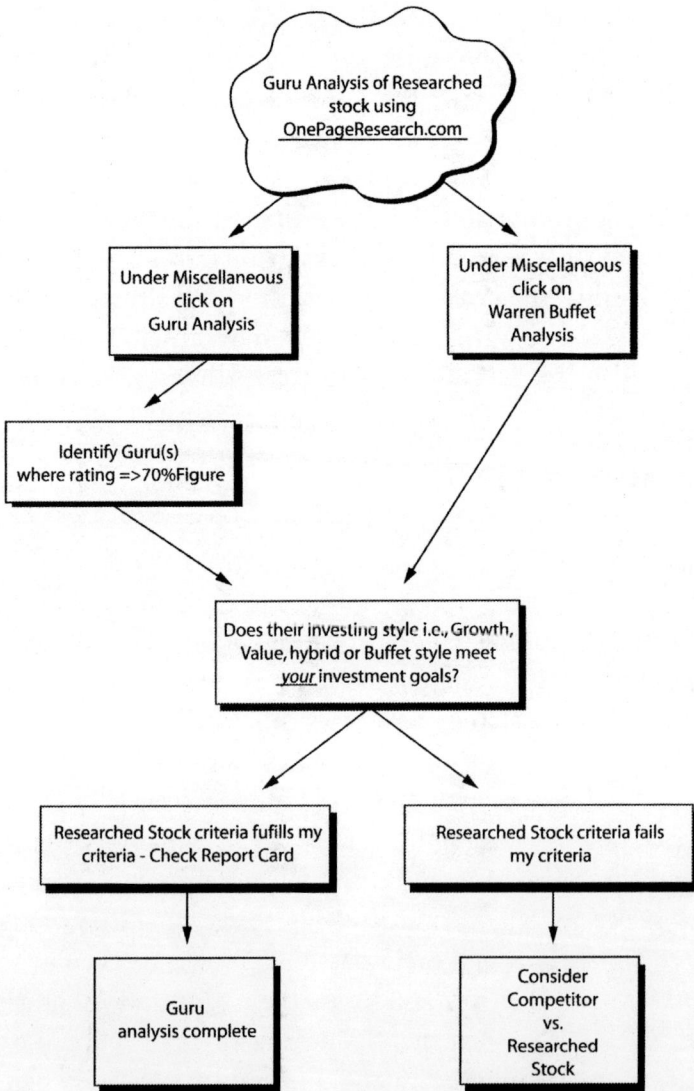

Figure 6. Guru Analysis

If you would now like to see if your stock pick passes the test of the fabled gurus above, using One Page Research will make it easier for you. I have provided simple way to view how these gurus might analyze your selection so you can compare their own personal evaluation criteria to your selected stock. (See Figure 6.)

Growth Stock Managers

Looking to see if your growth stock measures up? If so, then ask yourself the following question. How does my stock compare in the eyes of growth investors like Peter Lynch, William O'Neil, or Martin Zweig? Certainly one can select any percentage of scoring or rating, but I would recommend that the gurus rating for your stock be equal or greater than seventy percent to qualify in meeting the gurus guidelines and gaining a passing score. Observing the report card and detailed analysis for each guru will provide the individual investor with valuable analytical information about how their company compares with the guru's own detailed benchmarks about your selected stock.

Looking for a growth stock to add to your portfolio, then ask yourself this question. How does my stock compare in the eyes of investors like Peter Lynch, William O'Neil, or Martin Zweig, known for spotting successful growth stocks early? Use the flow diagram in Figure 6 to see what percentage or rating your stock yields from your favorite guru. For me, a stock has to have a rating of equal to or greater than seventy percent to say that it passes a guru strategy guidelines. Looking at their report card for a nicely detailed analysis from each guru. This will provide individual investors valuable analytical information and insight about their own stock picking focus.

Value Stock Managers…

Conversely, let's say you think you have identified a value stock for inclusion into your portfolio. How does it compare to those value criterion of investors like Benjamin Graham, Kenneth Fisher or hybrid (growth and value) investor, James O'Shaugnessey? Just as with growth stocks, I would state that my stock's rating must be equal to or greater than seventy percent before saying it passes a guru strategy guidelines.

Warren Buffett…a Breed Apart

Warren Buffett is one of the most legendary modern day investors. His stringent investing guidelines cross both growth and value paths. Although one may not totally agree with his investing philosophy, he is irrefutably one of the best long-term successful investors of the twentieth century. His personal investing philosophy is only to invest in a company whose business model he fully understands. In addition, the company must have a well-known brand, sustainable business in good times and bad, be consistently profitable, and growing over many years. If you would like to see how your stock fares through his glasses, then follow guidelines in Figure 6.

Conclusion—From Buy and Hold, to Buy and Periodically Re-evaluate

Investors have seen a paradigm shift in information available about financial markets available on the Internet. Our efficient capital markets have created this phenomena and the individual investor is the prime beneficiary. As short as five years ago, financial analyst information was unavailable unless through a broker delivered by mail, fax or by hand. The same information is now online. In addition, news stories, corporate earnings, revenue and earnings are a mouse click away or easily found on your PDA or web-enabled cellular phones. The most profound change occurred just in the year 2001. It was called SEC Regulation FD[48]. This totally leveled the playing field for access to time sensitive information between analysts and individual investors. No longer are financial analysts privileged with special guidance from corporations unless the same material is disseminated in the news media for instant access.

Perhaps an individual investor's greatest challenge is for self-reliance in matters of equity research, decision making and monitoring of their stock portfolios. One Page Research came into existence initially as a tool for use by the authors and friends. However, over time it has evolved to consolidate essential equity research using financial Internet resource links on a single web page.

As I close this chapter, the time-honored buy and hold strategy has been replaced by a new investment schema of investment strategy. The new strategy follows careful research for potentially winning stocks with due diligence. After making a decision to buy, periodically reevaluate to either hold (and watch the price slowly appreciate) or sell. Of course this decision depends upon the fundamentals staying intact with the price chart hopefully improving. Periodically following the Quick Scan (See Figure 2) method, individuals should be able to provide their own due diligence any time and anywhere access to the Net is available. The direct result for investors will be to become masters of their own portfolio and take charge of their own investments. Making this

---

48 On December 20, 1999, the Commission proposed new Regulation FD – for "fair disclosure"–to combat selective disclosure. Selective disclosure occurs when issuers release material nonpublic information about a company to selected persons, such as securities analysts or institutional investors, before disclosing the information to the general public. This practice undermines the integrity of the securities markets and reduces investor confidence in the fairness of those markets. (*www.sec.gov*)

process easy to follow has been the goal of this chapter. The use of simple algorithms for decision making in the sphere of fundamental, technical, competitor and guru analysis should be part of every investor's tool box for stock research and analysis.

Epilogue

It was the desire of the authors to create a book targeted to the beginning investor who uses the Internet and wishes to learn about equity research. With so many vast and diverse education sources on the Net, we have tried to create a user-friendly Web site associated with this book. Thus, One Page Research® evolved with links to the favorite sites of the authors, providing key information necessary for equity research.

Hopefully, this book has educated the reader to learn the basics of Confirmatory Analysis® while presenting a solid foundation of understanding in the areas of fundamental and technical analysis, and providing tools and approaches to technology investing.

Financial markets and leadership stocks are ever changing. When one style of investing fades (i.e., markets favoring only growth), the pendulum often swings to the other extreme, (i.e., value), and vice versa. Learning the basics of stock screening and defining criteria for any style of investing should now be easier for the individual investor and allow him/her to identify winning stocks for his/her portfolio.

Interestingly enough, during the final stages of manuscript editing during the summer of 2001, copy editor Nathan Taylor applied the Confirmatory Analysis principles for screening stocks and evaluating charts and came across MDCI (Medical Action Industries). Just like Ultrak, here was a stock that exhibited very strong fundamentals, a good price pattern, and was below the radar screen of institutional investors. How has it fared? The reader is directed to find a chart from the time frame of this book until the present for the answer.

Gaining wisdom and success in investing is a function of experience both making and losing money in the market. If you would like a daily Investor's Quote of the Day™ from The Little Investing Book™, then log onto *www.littleinvestingbook.com*. You may access these quotations from the web, through a PDA (Personal Digital Assistant) using the Palm OS® Web Clipping Technology over a Palm.Net wireless palm device (Palm VII or equivalent), or if your PDA isn't wireless, by downloading the AvantGo web browser from *www.avantgo.com*. The print version of the book is currently under development.

The authors disclaim any guarantee of success using the methods, web sites, and methodologies presented in this book.

About the Authors

Richard Davis, M.D., M.B.A. is now a retired Board Certified physician. Known to his friends as the Stockdoctor™ because of his keen interest in equity markets and being a physician, he works with others in educating them in reaching their investing goals.

James E. Farris, Ed.D. is currently Vice President of Medical Education for Baptist Hospital in Nashville, TN. His long time friendship and investing interest with the authors coupled with his professional background in educational methodology has greatly assisted others in pursuing their own personal investment education process.

Allan P. Harris, J.D. is a full time trader living on Kiawah Island, South Carolina. Retired from the practice of law in 1994, he lives in Kiawah year round with his first love, his family, pursuing his second love, stock trading using technical analysis, primarily in the form of assorted pattern recognition techniques.

Glossary

Accretion—Asset growth, by external expansion or acquisition; produces increasing EPS.

American Depository Receipts (ADRs)—Negotiable certificates issued by a U.S. bank representing a specific number of shares of a foreign stock traded on a New York Stock Exchange. Companies must confirm to U.S. FASB (Financial Accounting Standards Bureau) in order to be listed as an ADR.

Balance Asset Sheets—A quantitative summary of a company's financial condition at a specific point in time, including assets, liabilities and net worth. Also called statement of condition.

Bollinger Bands—A technical analysis chart trend described by John Bollinger using moving averages. Bollinger Bands are plotted as plus or minus 2 standard deviations over a 200 day moving average based on closing prices.

Bottom Line Earnings—Gross sales minus taxes, interest, depreciation, and other expenses. Also called net earnings or net income.

Capital Structure—The permanent long-term financing of a company, including long-term debt, common stock and preferred stock, and retained earnings. It differs from financial structure, which includes short-term debt and accounts payable.

Cash Flow Analysis—A method of evaluating an investment by estimating future cash flows and taking into consideration the time value of money. Also called capitalization of income.

Cost of Goods Sold (CGS)—On an income statement, the cost of purchasing raw materials and manufacturing finished products. Equal to the beginning inventory plus the cost of goods purchased during some period minus the ending inventory. Also called cost of sales.

Current Ratio (CR)—Current assets divided by current liabilities. An indication of a company's ability to meet short-term debt obligations; the higher the ratio, the more liquid the company is.

Dividends—A taxable payment declared by a company's board of directors and given to its shareholders out of the company's current or retained earnings. Usually quarterly. Usually given as cash (cash dividend), but it can also take the form of stock (stock dividend) or other property. Also called payout.

Downtrend—Downward price movement of a security or the overall market. Opposite of uptrend.

Earnings Per Share (EPS)—Total earnings divided by the number of shares outstanding. Companies often use a weighted average of outstanding stock over the reporting term.

Economy of Scale—Reduction in cost per unit resulting from increased production, realized through operational efficiencies. The plural is economies of scale.

Efficient Capital Markets—Markets where information flows so readily that no investor has knowledge at any point in time ahead of others. The price of the stock reflects any public knowledge reflected in balance sheets, income statements, and dividend announcements.

Fiscal Year—An accounting period of 365 days (366 in leap years), but not necessarily starting on January 1.

Fundamentals—The basics, Return on Equity, sales, earnings growth, debt loss, current ratio of a company.

Fundamental Analysis—A method of security valuation which involves examining the company's financials and operations, especially sales, earnings, growth potential, assets, debt, management, products, and competition.

Gross Margins—Gross income divided by net sales, expressed as a percentage.

Initial Public Offering—The first sale of stock by a company to the public.

Insolvency—Unable to meet debt obligations. Opposite of solvent.

Institutional Surfing—The technique whereby money managers use The Data Monitor, a weekly published by William O'Neil & Co., which lists companies' stock performances, technical charts and shareholders.

Liquidity—The ability of an asset to be converted into cash quickly and without any price discount.

Marginal Cost—The selling price where all fixed and variable costs are included. Selling above marginal cost is profitable.

Market Maker—Brokerage companies who buy a large number of shares in a stock and resell them to individual investors. Carrying large blocks of stock in their inventory of overall holdings is often disclosed on stock transaction confirmations under the phrase, "We make a market in this stock."

Market Multiple—Aggregate earnings per share of the S&P 500 stocks, divided by the current S&P 500 Value. Historical average S&P 500 market multiple from 1950-present is 14 with a standard deviation of four; range is 7-23.

Market Share—The percentage of the total sales of a given type of product or service that are attributable to a given company.

Momentum—The perceived strength behind a price movement.

Oscillator—A technical analysis term for an indicator that moves up and down, wavelike, within a price range.

PEG Ratio—A stock's price/earnings ratio divided by its year-over-year earnings growth rate.

Price/Book Ratio—A stock's capitalization divided by its book value. The value is the same whether the calculation is done for the whole company or on a per share basis.

Price/Earnings Ratio—The most common measure of how expensive a stock is. Equal to a stock's capitalization divided by its after-tax earnings over a 12-month period, usually the trailing period but occasionally the current or forward period. The value is the same whether the calculation is done for the whole company or on a per share basis. Equivalently, the cost an investor in a given stock must pay per dollar of current annual earnings. Also called earnings multiple.

Price Pattern—Formation on a technical analysis chart showing recent price movements, used in an attempt to predict future price movements. Also called trading pattern.

Price/Sales Ratio—A stock's capitalization divided by its sales over the trailing 12 months. The value is the same whether the calculation is done for the whole company or on a per share basis.

Profitability—The ability to earn a profit.

Resistance—Inability of a stock to rise above a certain price (resistance level).

Restructuring—Reorganize a company's operations by selling assets, divisions of a company, or layoffs to improve the net income per share.

Retracement—A price movement in the opposite direction of the previous trend.

Return on Equity (ROE)—A measure of how well a company used reinvested earnings to generate additional earnings, equal to a fiscal year's after-tax income (after preferred stock dividends but before common stock dividends) divided by shareholders equity, expressed as a percentage.

Return on Assets (ROA)—A measure of a company's profitability, equal to a fiscal year's earnings divided by its total assets, expressed as a percentage.

Revenue—Total dollar amount collected for goods and services provided.

Securities—An investment instrument, other than an insurance policy or fixed annuity, issued by a corporation, government, or other organization which offers evidence of debt or equity.

Sideways Pattern—A price which is neither rising or falling; sometimes called flat.

Solvency—A company's ability to meet its short term obligations by its adequacy of liquid assets.

Stop/Loss Order—A stop order for which the specified price is below the current market price and the order is to sell.

Support—In technical analysis, a price level which a security has had difficulty falling below.

Technical Analysis—A method of evaluating securities by relying on the assumption that market data, such as charts of price, volume, and open interest, can help predict future (usually short-term) market trends. Unlike fundamental analysis, the intrinsic value of the security is not considered.

Uptrend—Upward price movement of a security or the overall market. Opposite of downtrend.

Trendline—Technical analysis formation created by drawing a line connecting a series of descending tops, descending bottoms, ascending tops or ascending bottoms. Some technical analysts look for prices breaking through trendlines on the belief that those stocks have broken through a resistance level and are headed in a new direction.

Whisper Number—Rumored earnings numbers about to be reported, especially when they differ from the consensus forecast.